Even Mystics Have Bills to Pay

Also by Jim Rosemergy

A Closer Walk With God
A Daily Guide to Spiritual Living
A Recent Revelation
Living the Mystical Life Today
The Watcher
The Sacred Human
The Transcendent Life
The Quest for Meaning: Living a Life of Purpose

EVEN MYSTICS HAVE BILLS TO PAY

Balancing
a Spiritual Life
and Earthly Living

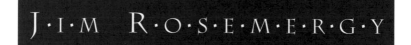

J·I·M R·O·S·E·M·E·R·G·Y

Unity House

Unity Village, Missouri

First Unity House Edition 2000

Unity House is a publishing imprint of Unity School of Christianity. To receive a catalog of all Unity publications (books, cassettes, compact discs, and magazines) or to place an order, call the Customer Service Department: 816-969-2069 or 1-800-669-0282.

The publisher wishes to acknowledge the editorial work of Raymond Teague, Michael Maday, and Medini Longwell; the copy services of Kay Thomure, Beth Anderson, and Marlene Barry; the production help of Rozanne Devine and Jane Blackwood; and the marketing efforts of Allen Liles, Jenee Meyer, and Sharon Sartin.

Cover design by Gretchen West
Cover photo by © Daryl Benson/MASTERFILE
Interior design by Coleridge Design

The Revised Standard Version is used for all Bible verses, unless otherwise stated.

Library of Congress Card Number 99–67068
ISBN 0–87159-262-2
Canada BN 13252 9033 RT

Unity House feels a sacred trust to be a healing presence in the world. By printing with biodegradable soybean ink on recycled paper, we believe we are doing our part to be wise stewards of our Earth's resources.

TABLE OF

CONTENTS

INTRODUCTION

The work ethic used to work. It served past generations well. They made the ends meet. *"Work hard and you'll get ahead."* Effort alone prospered many families, but not anymore. People who once prospered are now homeless. More and more children are living below the poverty level. Industries that once supported successive generations are shutting down. Throughout most of the twentieth century, one person in the household worked and provided for the needs of the family. Now both husband and wife often work to ensure a basic standard of living. In election years, the incumbent politicians used to be able to prop up the economy so it looked good by election day, but there are times when it seems they are not able to perform the magic anymore.

This is not the time to redouble our efforts and to do what we have always done a little better. The old methods will not work. We are being called to a new way of life. Humanity has only scratched the surface of prosperous living. Now is the time to dig deeper, not for precious metals, but for the treasure that is within us. The issue is not a continuous supply of bread, but whether we will discover, "Man

1

shall not live by bread alone" (Mt. 4:4). This is the discovery made by the mystics of the world. They found that the food which nourishes our souls will also provide for our bodies and other human needs. Earthly food only feeds the body, but the fruit of Spirit animates body and soul.

Because these seekers of the Infinite were so completely committed to God, there is a tendency to think that they had forsaken the world. The Truth is they did not really turn from the world because even mystics have bills to pay; they turned toward God.

There are many reasons to admire and emulate the mystics. Perhaps the most compelling reason is that they found balance. By seeking the kingdom, they learned how to put earthly matters in perspective. By putting God first, they assigned the world its proper place.

Mystics are in the world, but not of it. Their security and sense of identity are not rooted in the earth, although they eat the grains and fruit of the harvest. They drink from the spring of living water Jesus revealed to the Samaritan woman, and they also drink the water for which all people thirst again and again.

Seeking God is difficult. Every mystic retreats from the world in order to gain perspective and to receive insights, revelations, and a new vision. Most of us will not consistently retreat from the world, but we have the same inner yearning to know our Creator and to let the Spirit of God do Its sacred work in and through and as us. We have families to support and things to accomplish that we value and feel are important. However, I believe we, too, can find the balance that many of the mystics found. Together we are joined in the sacred quest of the Infinite and in the fact that we have bills to pay. This is the common ground we tread. Spirit and Earth are intertwined with one another. Let us not consider the quest sacred and the paying of bills mundane and of little consequence. Let us render unto God the things that are God's and also live responsibly by paying our bills.

We feel the weight of worldly matters, but we also hear the call to come up higher. Let us respond not by living apart and isolating ourselves from the human family and the world, but by seeing earthly matters from a higher point of view. In this way, we will not forsake the world; we will assign it its proper place.

This is a grand undertaking. We are going to become monks of the city. Like the mystics of old, we will give ourselves to God. We will also look and act like the typical man or woman, but our values and the way we live will provide hints of a higher calling.

Let us tell few people what we believe. Instead, let us quietly pursue our relationship with the Presence. With diligence and with courage, let us put to the test the spiritual principles that promise true security and well-being. And then if individuals ask us about our way of life, it will not be because of what we have said; it will be because of what they have observed us doing.

A new life awaits us—one filled with security and well-being. Our watchword is balance. We are rich in Spirit, and our needs are met without making them the reason for our existence. God is at the center of our lives, and from this center, a perfect circle is drawn that does not forsake the world. Within this circle, all is sacred and a new vision is born which sees that even in the winter "the fields are already white for harvest" (Jn. 4:35).

SECTION ONE

The Foundation

Everything that stands has a foundation. A life of security and well-being is lived according to certain truths and principles. Like the load-bearing pillars of a great temple, they come first. Their strength allows the rest of the temple to be built, and it is their hidden presence in the completed temple that shelters those who dwell therein.

The first seven chapters of *Even Mystics Have Bills to Pay* are the foundation pillars of a prosperous life. Many of the principles will be familiar. They are like old friends. Easily we embrace them and acknowledge their worth. Other ideas will be new. In some instances, we will immediately see that they are necessary for the new life we are building. However, some of the principles may seem to contradict truths we have held dear. Let us not discount what appears new or strange. The ideals lived by the mystics were often not those lived by most of humanity. Persist, raise up the pillars, and the temple that is destined to be your new life will rise as well.

CHAPTER
1

But I've Got Needs!

When our son Ben was young and struggling to learn the importance of saving money, he ran out of funds at the same time he found a video game he thought he had to have. Ben asked Nancy and me for the money to buy the game. We declined his request, and he cried out: "But I've got needs. I've got needs!"

This is the cry of nearly every human being. "I've got needs." Understandably, our focus has been filling these needs. Long ago in human history, our survival depended upon meeting the needs of shelter, food, and water. Members of our human family still struggle with these necessities, but others have needs that they consider to be nearly as essential. The perceived needs may not determine our survival, but they affect our quality of life and the way we see ourselves—successful or unsuccessful. There is much at stake, so we spend many hours trying to build the resources necessary for our physical survival, security, self-esteem, and enjoyment.

We think we begin the journey to prosperous living when we answer the world's call to get a good job—with benefits. This, we are told, requires an education or specialized training, so schooling comes next. Finally, we are employed, so we can receive society's current medium of exchange—money. With enough coin and currency, the ends meet.

What a tragic story. It is more fable than Truth. Many of us are exhausted and disillusioned because we have tried to bring the fable to life. When we become characters in this story, we do not get ahead: we fall behind. This is natural when our focus and life's direction are trying to get what we do not have.

Needs Are Not the Real Issue

Needs are not the real issue. When we focus upon what we lack, we experience anxiety and a sense of inadequacy. At first there is hope, but it quickly dissipates in the face of another call from the creditor, an unexpected bill, a canceled order, or failed job interview. Focusing upon the need and trying to meet it are the methods of the past millennia. The new millennium demands that we put aside our needs. A life of quality does not begin with what is seemingly lacking. It begins as we turn our attention to what is present.

The Great Gift

Jesus was aware of the great gift lovingly extended to humanity. "It is your Father's good pleasure to give you the kingdom" (Lk. 12:32). Something is being offered to us—either we do not know what it is, how to recognize it, or how to receive it. The above scripture indicates that our wise Father created the universe and the laws which govern it in a way that supports our well-being and development.

Other earthly creatures experience the Father's pleasure. Years ago I lived in a climate with extremely cold winters. It was not unusual for the windchill to be tens of degrees below zero. Near my home there was a pony that lived outdoors in the elements. Each autumn he began to grow his thick winter coat. One cool November day, I stood at his corral and asked the pony where he got his warm winter coat. Did he purchase it at one of the local department stores? Was it a gift from someone? Did he find it beside the road? These were absurd questions, but the answer that rose in my mind conveyed a simple Truth. It came from within.

In a natural way, this creature of God was provided for and protected from the icy blasts of winter. It was the Father's good pleasure to provide the coat. It did not come through monumental effort. It was a natural expression of the pony. There was no struggle. He did not focus upon his need. He did not think about growing the coat. The pony was a pony, and his fur thickened for the winter just as surely as it would be shed in the spring.

This is a powerful lesson. It is akin to Jesus' words which are not only Truth, but sacred literature. "Therefore I tell you, do not be anxious about your life, what you shall eat or what you shall drink, nor about your body, what you shall put on. Is not life more than food, and the body more than clothing? Look at the birds of the air: they neither sow nor reap nor gather into barns, and yet your heavenly Father feeds them. Are you not of more value than they? And which of you by being anxious can add one cubit to his span of life? And why are you anxious about clothing? Consider the lilies of the field, how they grow; they neither toil nor spin; yet I tell you, even Solomon in all his glory was not arrayed like one of these. . . . But seek first his kingdom and his righteousness, and all these things shall be yours as well" (Mt. 6:25–29, 33). Our problem is that we toil and spin rather than seek the kingdom. It is the kingdom that is offered to us. It is more than the fulfillment of needs and dreams. It is what makes life meaningful.

The Promise

Jesus said the kingdom is like a pearl of great price, "who, on finding one pearl of great value, went and sold all that he had and bought it" (Mt. 13:46). What could be so valuable? The answer is *an aware-ness of God.* Spirit is the infinite source, but we experience the richness of Spirit when we awaken to the Presence. A promise is given. If we seek the kingdom of God and open ourselves to a conscious-ness of the Presence, our earthly needs will be met. We do not have to give them great attention.

It is time to accept the challenge of this promise and put the principle of seeking the kingdom to the test. It is time to determine if our earthly needs can be met without giving thought to them. The prom-ise has been fulfilled for others. Can it be fulfilled for us?

Do you remember the story of Eddie Rickenbacker, the World War I combat pilot and ace? During World War II, while on a special mission, he and his crew were shot down by enemy fire. For days they drifted at sea in a raft with only four small oranges to sustain them. They took turns reading from a small Bible one of the men carried. On the eighth day these words were read: "But seek first his king-dom and his righteousness, and all these things shall be yours as well" (Mt. 6:33). Within an hour, a seagull landed on Rickenbacker's head. He grabbed it, and they had food. Later a rain shower came, and they had water. They sought the kingdom, and their needs were met. Faith rose up in them, and it enabled the downed fliers to hang on for two more weeks before they were rescued.

Even in the most dire situation when the outlook is bleak, God remains our Creator, Sustainer, and Source. Surely our God is just, wise, and loving. If this is true, the universe and our very nature must be conceived in a way that provides for all of our needs. Our presence in the universe must be for a greater purpose than to be born, to have our earthly needs met, and to die. We are here as part of a grand design.

It is reasonable to assume that earthly needs are fulfilled not as we give attention to them, but as we give attention to our purpose and God mission. Anything less gives undue importance to the material aspects of life. They must not be the center of our lives. Our work is to acknowledge God as the source and to awaken to the Presence.

The Bible is filled with stories in which God, the Source, provides for the needs of individuals. Scripture tells the story of Elijah who was alone in the wilderness and how the ravens fed him. This event is not much different from the story of Eddie Rickenbacker and his men. In each event, a winged creature, a creation of God, helped to meet the physical need.

God Does Not Fulfill Needs

Humanity has many needs. Millions of people starve to death each year. Why doesn't God help these people? Individuals who do not understand the nature of Spirit and how divine power is expressed turn from this seemingly harsh and uncaring God. This is particularly true when an individual has a need that is unfulfilled. This person asks: "Why doesn't God do something for me? I need a job. My children need coats and gloves for the winter." Once again we hear the cry of the human heart: "But I've got needs!"

The Truth is God does not fulfill needs. God is love itself. If God could fulfill a need, it would be done. No human being would ever lack for any good thing. From the human viewpoint, having God take care of our needs is a good plan. By the time you finish reading and working with this book, you will know a better plan—one conceived by Spirit—one that offers you riches you cannot even imagine at this moment.

The Open Door

Are you beginning to understand? We have needs. There is no doubt about this. Whole nations have needs. Continents have needs. From the human point of view, it seems reasonable that a loving and compassionate Creator would provide for the needs of Its creation. The Truth is our needs can be provided for, but not in the way we think. If God could fulfill a need, it would be done, but this is not the way the universe works. God cannot fulfill needs; the Source cannot express Itself through a need.

Notice that in the story of Elijah and the ravens and Eddie Rickenbacker and the gull, God did not act through a consciousness of lack. Spirit acted through the spiritual consciousness that grew as Elijah, and Eddie Rickenbacker and his men turned away from their shortage to God.

Spirit needs a consciousness that is focused upon It rather than the problem. This is why the need is not the issue. A focus upon what we do not have leads to anxiety and a sense of inadequacy. When we give our attention to Spirit and allow an awareness of the Source to rise up in us, our needs are taken care of without making them the center of our focus. Two powerful ideas are the foundation of this book and our lives. First, God is our source. Second, a consciousness of God is our supply.

Is there a time when God is not our source? Is there a time when our consciousness of Spirit will not provide for us? People have prospered in the most trying times. The economic climate or the level of deprivation does not matter. When consciousness is unaffected by the rise and fall of national, global, or personal economic indicators, we prosper. Only an awareness of God grants this way of life. Is it any wonder that it is called the pearl of great price?

Key Ideas

1. Needs are not the issue.
2. God has a plan that makes life meaningful and provides for our earthly needs.
3. The pearl of great price is an awareness of God.
4. Our earthly needs are met not as we give attention to them, but as we give attention to God.
5. God does not fulfill needs.
6. God is our source.
7. A consciousness of God is our supply.

Affirmation

I put to the test the great promise: Seek first the kingdom.

Summary

I put aside my needs and give my attention to God.

CHAPTER
2

Knowing What to Ask For

The Land of Sand

You are walking in a field of lilies toward a distant village you see nestled at the foot of a mountain. Everywhere you look there are gold nuggets. You pick up so many pieces of the precious metal that walking becomes a burden, but you are unwilling to let go of your new-found treasure. Burdened with new wealth, you enter the village believing you are richer than you have ever been in your life.

You have traveled for miles and are hungry and tired and need a place to stay. A villager gives you directions to a small inn. Upon entering, you approach the registration desk. Placing a small gold nugget on the counter, you ask for a room. The clerk looks at you and then the nugget and says, "I hope you are not going to try to pay for your room with that worthless rock."

After much discussion, you discover that gold has no value in this land. Sand is the medium of exchange, and you have none. Nor is it easy to find or acquire.

In order to prosper in the land of sand, you have to change your beliefs about what is valuable. In order to live in the kingdom of God, you have to discover the riches of Spirit. In the kingdom, neither sand nor gold nor money is the medium of exchange. Another "currency" is required.

Another Currency

Intuitively, we know this other currency. Even the smallest coin in America has imprinted upon it a statement that promises another way of life: "In God we trust."

In the world, we can be without money and have no clear means of acquiring it, but our wise God has devised a universe in which true riches are available to all. We can be adrift at sea, unemployed, or destitute, and the Source is present. In Truth, we carry it with us. When this treasure is unknown to us, it is like having a precious pearl sewn into the lining of our coat pocket and not knowing it is there.

We can say we trust in God, but more is required.

We must awaken to the Presence. God is not supply. God is our source. A consciousness of God is supply. This subtle difference accounts for much misunderstanding of the spiritual realm. Remember, God does not act through needs. The open door which allows the expression of divine power is spiritual consciousness, an awareness of God.

In the physical world, we must know what the supply is—money, gold, or sand—and then acquire it. Earthly supply is valuable because it is scarce. Not everybody has it. If everybody did, it would not be valuable. For this reason, it is helpful to store the supply for future use. This is humanity's plan.

The Divine Plan

The divine plan is this: A consciousness of God is supply. This awareness brings us security and well-being. The divine supply, an awareness of God, is available to everyone. It is not scarce. It can never be depleted; therefore, it does not need to be stored for future use. One has only to experience God as supply, and daily bread is provided.

God's plan requires an awareness of what is valuable, then needs are met. Awareness and acquisition are one. Under God's model, it would be foolish to give attention to the need. A deepened, more vivid awareness of the need only creates anxiety and a sense of inadequacy. A deepened awareness of God

grants us security and well-being as well as provides for our earthly needs. We do not have to make
earthly matters the focus of our lives. We have a
greater purpose.

The divine supply is available to all. Earthly riches
are not. Some countries have vast natural resources.
Others are barren. Some people are born into poverty and others into nobility. We are not born equal,
but we are created equal, for we have the capacity
to awaken to the presence of God.

Earthly economics say we can hold supply in our
hands and house it in banks and barns. The divine
supply rests perpetually within us as a part of our
spiritual nature. Through our attention, expectation,
and faith, we open ourselves to a consciousness of
Spirit.

Coin of the Realm

The coin of the heavenly realm, a consciousness
of God, does not depend upon our level of education or human abilities. People experienced security and well-being long before the first school of
learning ever came into being. Is it any wonder that
Jesus said, "I have food to eat of which you do not
know" (Jn. 4:32)?

In an earthly sense, both rich and poor fail to par-
take of the meat that is offered. They share the same
myth, the same erroneous ideas about supply. They

see money as the source; therefore, neither group of people sits at the banquet table that is prepared for humanity.

The rich in Spirit know that money is not supply. They may possess vast sums of money, or they may have little. One thing is certain—these rich ones have security and well-being that do not rise and fall with human circumstance. Something besides money stands under them as a foundation of true prosperity. Their substance (*substance* means that which stands under) is spiritual consciousness. These rich ones live in the kingdom of heaven.

The Sign of the Kingdom

There is a way to tell if we have entered the kingdom of heaven and found the pearl of great price. *Asking ceases.* Thomas Merton, a twentieth-century monk and mystic, believed that a rich man has no needs. On one level, this is obvious. Of course the rich have no needs, for they can have whatever they want. However, when we examine the lives of some of the earthly rich, it is obvious that some of their most basic needs are unfulfilled. For instance, in the twentieth century, Howard Hughes was one of the wealthiest men on Earth, and yet he died in isolation and fear.

Thomas Merton is alluding to the enlightenment that occurs when we are consciously one with God.

Our asking ceases because we are fulfilled. In that moment, there is nothing that we need. We have God. What else could we want? This is true riches. In a later chapter, we will explore the journey to no-needs.

As long as we are asking to have our needs met, we have not met our Creator. When we experience our oneness with Spirit, in that moment, asking ceases.

Supply=Demand

The world functions under the premise of supply and demand. In the kingdom of heaven, in spiritual consciousness, the principle is supply equals demand. Supply is God's side of the formula. Demand is our side; so we demand, but nothing happens. We have asked for a new job and a healing, but the bills continue to mount up and the pain endures. The scripture says, "Ask, and it will be given you; seek, and you will find; knock, and it will be opened to you" (Mt. 7:7). Is this a promise or a lie?

It is the Truth. Supply does equal demand, but we "ask amiss" (Jas. 4:3 KJV). We have asked for earthly things, but it is God we want. This is our deepest heart's desire. Let us ask for God. This is a request Spirit always fulfills. Then a new life opens to us. Job opportunities may come. Our bodies may be restored, but there is a greater joy, a boundless joy, that comes when we know what to ask for.

Key Ideas

1. A consciousness of God is supply.
2. Divine supply, an awareness of God, is available to everyone.
3. Divine supply does not need to be stored for future use.
4. Divine supply is never depleted.
5. Awareness and acquisition are one.
6. A deepened awareness of God grants us security and well-being as well as provides for our earthly needs.
7. A consciousness of God does not depend upon our level of education or human abilities.
8. Supply equals demand.
9. As long as we ask to have our needs met, we have not met our Creator.
10. A new life opens to us when we ask for an awareness of God.

Affirmation

I ask for God.

Summary

Supply is a consciousness of Spirit.

CHAPTER
3

What's Your Penny?

When Antoinette Bourignan was eighteen years old, she yearned for God, but the world was pressing in upon her. As was the practice in the seventeenth century, a marriage was arranged for her, but she longed to be the bride of the Christ. At a young age, she gave herself to God. At four o'clock one morning, she dressed herself as a hermit, took one penny to buy a day's bread, and left her home. As she departed, the still, small voice said to her: "Where is your faith? In a penny?" These words touched her, and she released her hold on the penny. By throwing it away, Antoinette continued not only her earthly travels, but her journey into the kingdom of God.

As the still, small voice spoke to Antoinette, she realized the penny was a symbol of her dependence

upon earthly things and a barrier to her realization
of the Source. Therefore, she cast the penny aside.
It may have bought bread for a day, but what about
the days to follow? The spent penny would not help
her tomorrow. Only an awareness of the Source
could provide for her on the days to come.

Remember, God is willing, and it is the Father's
good pleasure to give us the kingdom. The kingdom
is here, at hand, within our grasp, but we hold on
to other things. We believe they contribute to our
security, but they do not. Just as we cannot serve
two masters, so we cannot hold to earthly things
and the kingdom and call both of them our source.

What is your penny? What earthly things do you
mistakenly believe make you safe and secure? What
barriers have you erected between you and the riches
that are yours in spiritual consciousness? There are
many possibilities.

Humanity's Pennies

Antoinette Bourignan took one penny when she
left home on her spiritual journey. When we begin
the same pilgrimage, we initially carry at least three
pennies. Each one must be discarded.

In the nineteenth century, there were many
theories about the source of the Nile. Numerous
explorers failed in their search for the headwaters.
Finally after arduous journeys, John Hanning Speke

(1827–64) discovered not a trickle of water high in the mountains, but a vast source of seemingly limitless water—Lake Victoria. We have a similar discovery to make.

When an explorer travels in Africa, many provisions are needed for the expedition. They are not a burden, for they sustain the traveler on a day-to-day basis. Our journey is different. Many of the "provisions" that we carry and view as essential are actually burdens to be shed before the unlimited riches of the Presence are discovered. Let us look into our pockets, and we will find not a copper coin, but a false way of seeing. The first penny humanity must discard if it is to experience the riches that are ours in God is judging by appearances. The second is thinking lack, and the third is holding resentments toward ourselves and others. No one enters the kingdom of God or finds security and well-being when these three coins jingle in his or her pockets.

Judging by Appearances

The classic human error is judging by appearances. Lack of vision hides the Truth of Being from us in so many areas of human experience. This is especially true when it comes to prosperity. We falsely believe that people are our source. This begins in childhood when our parents provide for our needs. Most likely many children have heard their parents discussing money and talking about how the lack of money created problems for the family. Conversely, it is easy for a child to believe that money brings happiness. Often the more money someone has, the more "stuff" the person acquires.

As we grow older and begin our careers, money remains the source, but we no longer look to our parents. We look to our employers, the government, or customers. When we retire, the source is social security, a pension plan, or our investments. Of course, money can come through various channels. It may be held as land, stocks, or precious metals, but essentially, we must have enough of a valuable thing, and then we are safe and secure.

In biblical times there was a practice called the Jubilee Year. It came every fifty years. Land was a valuable commodity during those days, but during the Jubilee Year, something remarkable happened. Land was returned to its previous owner. No one owned the same land for more than fifty years. Eventually, the revelation came upon the people that the Earth was the Lord's.

What if every fifty years we had to empty our bank accounts and give away our assets? We would certainly discover the meaning of giving and receiving. No one would make "making money" his or her life's work. Other priorities would dominate our lives. Money would not be as valuable as we currently make it. In Truth, we would discover true wealth to be a consciousness of God. As long as we had this, we would be safe and secure.

Let us cast aside the penny that declares something or someone other than God as our source. As we do, we, like Antoinette, can continue our journey into the kingdom. Let us listen in the quietness of our souls, and we will hear the still, small voice saying: "Where is your faith? In a penny? In your job? In your pension plan? In the government? In a person?" Will we cast aside this penny?

Thinking Lack

When we believe something other than a consciousness of God is our supply, we eventually hold in mind thoughts of lack and limitation. Because thinking lack produces lack, even what we have is lost. It is as Jesus said, "from him who has not, even what he has will be taken away" (Mt. 25:29). The have-not consciousness can produce only one thing—loss. I once had a friend who experienced deprivation and lack with great regularity. Often I told him that he was looking at the hole in the donut. There were blessings in his life, but during the darkest times, his attention was upon what he did not have—what he lacked. This was his focus and what he manifested in his life—loss. If his utility bill was one hundred and twenty dollars, and he received a gift of one hundred dollars, he would not bless and give thanks for the gift. He would look at what he did not have, the needed twenty dollars.

Myth declares that before the time of recorded history, there was a king whose thoughts more than his actions governed the land and influenced the people. When the king was in a positive frame of mind, the crops flourished, wars ceased, and open trade with other lands prospered the people. When the king was troubled and his thoughts turned negative, a darkness spread across the land. Wars erupted, natural disasters occurred, rains ceased, and food was scarce. During these times, the king was given positive stories to read, and the court jesters and magicians tried to cheer the monarch. For a time they would be successful, but then darkness would come again.

Eventually, the king visited a wise sage revered by the people. He told the wise one of his love for his people and how they tried to help him, but that his joy was fleeting when it came from their actions or from a book. The sage said the king was like anyone except that his thoughts influenced not only his own life, but the life of the land and its people.

"The answer," the sage said, "is not in amusement or filling the mind with positive thoughts. It is to tap the wellspring of goodness that lies within. That which is already within you will rise up and bless you, the people, and the land."

The penny that represents a consciousness of lack

is not easily tossed aside. Nor can we simply think positively, and all will be well. Thoughts are not the real shape formers of our lives; it is thought patterns woven together that form our consciousness. These are the builders of our life experiences. We can try to cease thinking negatively and fill our minds with positive thoughts. We can guard our thoughts and try to speak only positive words. We may try to live this dream, but our thoughts betray us. They are not all positive even though we know the impact that negative thinking has upon our experiences. This guarding of our thoughts can become its own prison. Positive thinking is a good beginning and part of a rite of passage, but there is a more excellent way. A consciousness of the Source must rise up from within us. Then we are free.

Mystical lore speaks of watering a garden. We can carry water to the individual plants and the garden will grow, but it is laborious work. Another option is to construct irrigation canals and send the water from a nearby stream to our garden, and it will begin to thrive. But a garden is watered best when it rains. This is God's way—an awareness of the Source rising from within like a shower upon a parched land. In the chapters to come, we will address the building of the irrigation system and how to invite the rain. When the rain comes, we will cast aside the penny of negative thinking which denies us a prosperous life.

Holding Resentments

God is our source, and a consciousness of God is our supply; however, resentment stands as a barrier to prosperity. God is Love, but when we are filled with resentment and anger, we cannot feel the love that is our nature and that perpetually enfolds us. Anything that shields us from a consciousness of God separates us from our supply.

In the Lord's Prayer, Jesus said, "And forgive us our debts, as we also have forgiven our debtors" (Mt. 6:12). It appears this verse says that God does not forgive us as long as we do not forgive others. The Truth is God does not forgive because God is Love. There is no resentment in God. However, the verse stresses an important idea. As long as we fail to forgive, we are not able to experience the love God is. Through a consciousness of love, we are cared for and our earthly needs are met.

Our destiny is oneness with Spirit. We may want this experience and "offer our gift at the altar," but a relationship with God is not possible when we are unforgiving. "So if you are offering your gift at the altar, and there remember that your brother has something against you, leave your gift there before the altar and go; first be reconciled to your brother, and then come and offer your gift" (Mt. 5:23–24). Don't you love Jesus' tact? Notice how he says if you remember that *"your brother has something against you . . ."* Far be it that we might have something against our brother . . .

Not only does resentment shield us from the love God is, it also erects a barrier to powerful, loving relationships. We will not be able to perform our work with joy and great efficiency if we hold resentments toward others. Jesus stressed this idea when he said to the disciples, "And whatever town or village you enter, find out who is worthy in it, and stay with him until you depart. As you enter the house, salute it. And if the house is worthy, let your peace come upon it; but if it is not worthy, let your peace return to you. And if any one will not receive you or listen to your words, shake off the dust from your feet as you leave that house or town" (Mt. 10:11–14).

Jesus' words are relevant in many areas of life, but none more so than our professional lives. The disciples were called to a "professional" life of service. Some people would be receptive to their message, and others would not. If the disciples resented those who condemned them or persecuted them, the feelings of rejection and resentment would be carried to the next town and its people. Not only would the disciples be unable to experience the Presence, their unresolved resentments formed from past encounters would sabotage the work that was before them. Many people's careers are stifled because they cannot get along with their boss or co-workers. Because of undeveloped communication skills, they are unable to truly hear their coworkers and clients. This limitation makes success in the business world nearly impossible.

This is a vast subject we will examine in the chapters to follow, but let us make a covenant to be willing to cast aside this penny that stands between us and a prosperous life.

The Burden Is Light

The three coins of judging by appearances, thinking lack, and holding resentments can be discarded. They are not a natural part of life. Antoinette cast aside her penny and received the riches of God's presence. Our burden is heavier, but when it is tossed aside, the riches of the Presence are also ours. Let us rejoice, for we have begun. We are willing. This is enough for now. Through our willingness to cease judging by appearances, to stop thinking lack, and to shake the dust from our feet, our grip upon these coins is lessening. They are not yet cast aside, but the day of their release is at hand.

Key Ideas

1. Judging by appearances is a barrier to a consciousness of God.
2. Thinking lack is a barrier to a consciousness of God.

3. Holding resentments is a barrier to a consciousness of God.
4. Money is not our source or supply.
5. True wealth is an awareness of Spirit.
6. The have-not consciousness can produce only one thing—loss.
7. A consciousness of the Presence is destined to rise from within us.
8. Anything that shields us from a consciousness of God separates us from supply.

Affirmation

I release all that stands between me and an awareness of God.

Summary

I am willing to begin releasing resentment and thoughts of lack as well as judging by appearances.

CHAPTER
4

Are You Willing to Prosper?

It is the Father's good pleasure to give us the kingdom, but are we willing to receive? With our words, we say we want all that God has for us, but our closed hands betray us.

Often when I speak about prosperity, I begin the lesson by holding up fifty dollars and saying, "Who deserves this fifty dollar bill?" It is amazing, but only a few hands go up. I invite the first person I see with a raised hand to come forward and take the money. Then I say: "Why wasn't everyone's hand up? How do you expect to receive the wonders and riches of the kingdom of heaven if you do not believe you deserve fifty dollars?"

I remember doing the same thing at a direct-marketing sales meeting. These people planned to

prosper and envisioned themselves becoming rich.
Amazingly, when I offered the money, no one raised
a hand. After waiting in silence for someone to act,
my wife, who accompanied me, raised her hand. She
received the money.

One Closed Hand

The truth is that often we do not feel deserving.
We think we are unworthy, and therefore, in subtle
ways, we say no to God and to the most basic prosperity. Sometimes we carry a sense of guilt and
punish ourselves by refusing to receive. Since Spirit
does not force Itself upon us, there is nothing God
can do until we say yes. God waits until we raise
our hands.

In 2 Kings 4:1–7, there is a wonderful story about
the importance of receptivity. A man who used to
work for the prophet Elisha has died, and a creditor has come to take the widow's sons in payment
for a debt. Elisha arrived and asked the woman what
she had. She told him, "Your maidservant has nothing in the house, except a jar of oil." Obviously, she
considered the jar of oil meager and insufficient to
pay the debt. The man of God saw it differently. This
heavenly sight was the beginning of riches for the
woman and her sons.

Elisha said to the woman, "Go outside, borrow
vessels of all your neighbors, empty vessels and not

too few." The woman did as he said and returned with many containers. She then received additional instructions to close the door (shutting out any negative thoughts or people) and to pour the oil from the small flask into the many containers. The oil flowed continuously until there were no more containers. The message is clear. We receive according to our capacity to receive.

The story concludes with Elisha saying, "Go, sell the oil and pay your debts, and you and your sons can live on the rest." On the surface, the man of God told the woman she could live on the profits from the sale of the oil for the rest of her life, but this is not true. No prophet of God would consider money from the sale of oil to be true supply. The "rest" that would sustain the family was not money from the sale of oil, but the spiritual awareness that dawned in them. A person receives according to his or her capacity to receive. This insight is more valuable than precious metals, money, or oil.

Our receptivity is paramount. Spirit will not force Itself upon us, but it is the Father's good pleasure to give us the kingdom. The kingdom is an awareness of the Presence. It is our supply, but we do not know how to receive it. Often we do not even ask for it. We are too preoccupied with earthly matters. We fail to understand the nature of wealth, riches, and poverty. We cry out for supply, but our hands are closed.

Another Closed Hand

Humanity believes it is a blessing to be rich, but has attached a stigma to wealth. We wonder if the acquisition of wealth is "dirty business." Some people lower their values in order to get what they feel they must have. We question the way wealth is used. For some, it is power. For others, it is viewed as the way to happiness and security. Mansions and the outward show of opulence seem inappropriate in a world plagued with poverty and famine. It is not surprising that although we believe riches to be a blessing, we also wonder if they are a curse.

Is Poverty a Virtue?

The clergy used to teach that poverty was a virtue and riches a sin. Jesus seemed to reinforce this belief when he said, "It is easier for a camel to go through the eye of a needle than for a rich man to enter the kingdom of God" (Mk. 10:25). Oddly enough, even as the church endorsed this teaching, it was becoming one of the wealthiest institutions on Earth. History records that this was a time of corruption in the church and that many of the clergy were in collusion with the secular leaders.

The church did not condemn money and riches. Instead it stressed the virtue of poverty. The church promised glory and a better life after death. In fact, suffering in earthly experience bound one to Jesus, for it was taught he suffered for humanity. The kings and church profited from people's willingness to accept poverty and harsh conditions.

At this same time, there were mystics and aesthetes who also seemed to endorse the virtue of poverty. The aesthetic life demanded that one withdraw from the world and forsake all but the most basic necessities of earthly living. Poverty seemed virtuous. As is often the case with the mystics, we fail to understand the wisdom they lived. By going apart, these desert fathers, as they were called, discovered true riches.

This discovery lies before us now. Is it a "sin" to be rich? In our day and age, some say it is not a sin; it is a miracle. A good place to begin is with another question. What is it to be rich? Is it having money, precious metals, or land? Is it having what is scarce and valued by other people—oil, for instance? The Bedouins of Abraham's time considered many sons and vast herds to be signs of wealth.

The mystics had another insight. For these friends of God, richness was an awareness of the Presence. This is why a consciousness of God is supply. Because of this awareness, those heavy laden with gold were considered poor if they believed gold made them rich and secure.

The mystics never endorsed the poverty of malnutrition and deprivation. In Truth, they considered themselves rich because of their relationship with God. They considered people poor who thought themselves rich because of possessions.

These seekers of the infinite knew poverty was not a virtue. Poverty was a life without God rather than life without possessions. In simplicity, they found a relationship with the Presence. They illustrated by their lives that the issue is not earthly riches, but giving themselves to Spirit. When this work is done, we are blessed. The amount of money we have determines little. We may live in simplicity or be stewards of large amounts of wealth. The planet needs both kinds of people. Those who live in simplicity teach us that happiness lives in us rather than in circumstances. The stewards of vast earthly wealth who have a deep relationship with Spirit help us with our physical needs and in the discovery of our self-worth.

Another Sign of Wealth

The question is, What will we do with what we have? This is another way of determining wealth. Imagine an individual with a brilliant mind. He or she can memorize facts and possess great knowledge. Does this make the person wise? Isn't wisdom the application of knowledge?

When resources are used only for ourselves, no matter how much money we have, we are not rich.

When we are a blessing to the world, we are rich no matter what we give. Many years ago *Reader's Digest* published a story about Thomas Cannon, a postal worker who lived on a salary of less than $17,000 a year, but over the course of ten years he gave $35,000 to many worthy causes. He adjusted his lifestyle, so he could give in the way that he wanted to give.

John Templeton is a wealthy financier who helped manage billions of dollars. However, he is more than wealthy in an earthly sense; he is rich in Spirit. Mr. Templeton understands the value of spirituality. In fact, he has conceived an award that honors and financially rewards individuals who contribute to the spiritual unfoldment of humankind. (Mother Teresa and Billy Graham are among awardees.) Mr. Templeton's award is greater in value than the Nobel Peace Prize because he feels spirituality is of greater value than peace. In fact, one flows from the other. The point is true that wealth is not a matter of what we have, but what we do with what we have. John Templeton and Thomas Cannon both know the riches of God.

For Love of Money

Some people mistakenly quote the Bible as saying that money is the root of all evil, when in fact the scripture declares, "For the love of money is the root of all evils" (1 Tim. 6:10). Money is not the culprit. It is like the power of the atom. It can be a blessing or a curse. Take a coin or bill of any denomination and hold it in your open hand. Observe how lifeless it is. Money is nothing without you. It can do nothing without the aid of a human being.

Imagine what the coin or currency can purchase. If you hold a penny, there is little that it can buy in today's American economy. However, in other economies it has a greater purchasing power. Periodically, we receive literature which tells us that a small donation can feed a child in another land for one month.

Basically, money is a medium of exchange that has made the barter system obsolete. Thank God! Imagine having to carry our goods from store to store and bargain with merchants for the necessities of life. Money is a matter of convenience, and as we shall see, a symbol of the unlimited supply.

What is the real power behind money? Our federal government ensures its viability. In the past, our economic system was backed by gold. Theoretically, a dollar could be redeemed for a specific amount of gold. This is no longer true, but our government remains the foundation of our monetary system. Or is it? Actually, the confidence of the people in the government is the foundation. Without our confidence, the coins and currency are worth little.

During the Civil War, the confederacy printed

money, but it took a wheelbarrow load to purchase the items necessary for a week's food for a family. The people lost confidence in the government, and the currency became worthless.

Look again closely at the coin or bill you held in your hand. Special words are imprinted upon it— "In God we trust." God is our source and the foundation that supports not only our monetary system, but our lives.

Many years ago as a young minister, I was teaching my first prosperity class. During the class, I gave each person a dollar bill. In the audience was a man named Fred. He was just beginning his road to recovery from alcoholism. Fred took his dollar and kept it in his wallet as a symbol of his source. In the years to follow, Fred prospered in many ways. I can only imagine how many times Fred took that dollar from his wallet and looked at the inscription, "In God we trust." Perhaps he read the words in times of seeming limitation, and they gave him hope. Maybe as he prospered, he took the bill and read the inscription as a way of acknowledging his source and saying thanks. We can do the same.

Let us strike from our minds the idea that there is something wrong with earthly riches and something right about earthly poverty. Instinctively, we know this is not true. These attitudes are barriers to the richness that is a consciousness of God. Believe money and land make you rich, and you will know true poverty and insecurity. Believe God to be your source and a consciousness of God your supply, and you will experience true riches and well-being.

Key Ideas

1. It is the Father's good pleasure to give us the kingdom.
2. Poverty is believing that earthly things make us rich and secure.
3. Richness is an awareness of God.
4. We are poor when we do not have a relationship with God.
5. We are rich when God is our friend.
6. We receive according to our capacity to receive.
7. Richness is determined by what we do with what we have rather than by how much we have.
8. Money is a symbol of the unlimited supply.

Affirmation

I want to be rich in Spirit.

Summary

I willingly receive that which is the Father's good pleasure to give me—the kingdom of heaven.

CHAPTER
5

The Journey to No-Needs

Only the Rich Enter the Kingdom

Though Jesus said it is harder for a rich man to enter the kingdom of God than for a camel to go through the eye of a needle, in Truth only the rich can enter the kingdom. This statement does not contradict the wisdom of Jesus. It redefines what it is to be rich.

People usually describe wealth in terms of money. The disagreement is usually over how much money one must have to be considered rich. I counseled a man many years ago who said that he was wiped out financially and had only twenty thousand dollars in the bank. I listened intently, because at the time my family had about three hundred dollars in our account. He had twenty thousand dollars and was devastated. We had three hundred dollars and felt secure. Polls say that some people believe a person is rich when he or she makes a yearly income of one hundred and fifty thousand dollars. For some, being rich requires far less money while for others, much more.

The No-Need State

In Chapter 2, we discovered that a mystic "measures" riches in another way. When we are still and experience the Presence, we enter a state of consciousness where there are no needs. There is nothing we require. How could we? We have God, and God has us. The two are one. Asking ceases, for contentment and fulfillment inhabit the soul. The desire to ask God for anything indicates we have not entered the no-need state. We are outside the kingdom.

This is a great challenge for a human being, for often needs rule the day. Constantly, we are confronted by what we think we need but do not have. Food, drink, and shelter are needed for the body. Companionship is desired. We want a reason for being, a purpose for our existence, a mission. These desires are natural, "and your Father knoweth that ye have need of these things" (Lk. 12:30 KJV).

However, divine wisdom declares: "Seek first his kingdom and his righteousness, and all these things shall be yours as well" (Mt. 6:33). We don't have to make them our reason for being. We are spiritual beings destined to give expression to the Infinite. All that God is pours from within us into our lives and the lives of others. This pursuit requires our attention even though the tug of the human condition is strong. The good news is that there is a balanced way of life in which we "render to Caesar the things that are Caesar's [the world], and to God the things that are God's" (Lk. 20:25). The key is the no-need state.

I Shall Not Want

David, the shepherd boy who became king, discovered this key as the words of what was to become the Twenty-Third Psalm filled his mind. The first verse of the psalm describes the no-need state. "The Lord is my shepherd, I shall not want." When we are consciously one with God, we *cannot* want. We have everything. There is nothing for which to ask.

This awareness is the herald of true riches and well-being. It is more than a feeling of security that gives us solace for the moment. It is evidence of a consciousness that we first feel as fulfillment, but which will, like any state of consciousness, manifest itself as our life experiences. Through it, our earthly needs are met.

The Fields Are White for Harvest

John 4:35 records Jesus' teaching his disciples this important spiritual principle. I speculate that Jesus was speaking to his disciples in the winter when the fields were barren. How surprised they must have been when Jesus stretched forth his hand to the wind-swept, desolate fields and said, "I tell you, lift up your eyes, and see how the fields are already white for harvest." How puzzled the disciples must have been. He speaks of the harvest when the fields are barren. Is he mad? No, he sees and knows what other people have yet to discover.

Every barren life has within it a bountiful harvest, but the seeds to be cast to the wind are not earthly. It is not even the seeds of positive thinking and expectancy. The harvest does not come by asking for what appears to be lacking, but by experiencing the no-need state that yields a bountiful harvest even in the winter.

The Treasure in Heaven

The no-need state with its gifts of contentment and fulfillment is our natural state. It can come upon us at any time, for it is an act of grace. We cannot

make it come, but we have our work to do to prepare the soil of the soul for this seed whose harvest
is security. At first it will come and go, but eventually it will remain as a constant companion.

Our work is to heed Jesus' counsel to lay up "treasures in heaven, where neither moth nor rust consumes and where thieves do not break in and steal"
(Mt. 6:20). This supply or consciousness which is
untouched by the human condition can provide for
us in the most dire situation.

Our first step is to purify our motivation. A can-
didate for the no-need state values a consciousness
of God above all, for this person knows it is supply.
God is the source, but it has no avenue of expression until we are conscious of the Presence. The odd
thing is that we know we are in the kingdom when
we, like the shepherd boy David, do not want.

Just as a desire to know God as our source and
to experience the no-need state is the beginning of
laying up treasures in heaven, so too is thanksgiving. "Enter his gates with thanksgiving, and his
courts with praise!" (Psalm 100:4) In olden times,
the people viewed God as a walled city. Perhaps
this was because they found it difficult to know
God, yet they viewed Spirit as a safe haven, a for-
tress. One of the issues of the day, just as it is in
modern times, is how to enter the city. Those who
came to know God found one of the gates to be
praise and thanksgiving.

"Thanksliving"

There are a number of ways to look at thanks-giving. When someone gives us something or does something nice for us, we say thank-you. This is courtesy, the simplest form of thanksgiving. Thanks-giving can also be an act of faith. We give thanks for something before it comes into being or before something happens. Jesus did this at Lazarus' tomb as he called Lazarus to come forth. "Father, I thank thee that thou hast heard me" (Jn. 11:41).

The third application of thanksgiving is a grand expression of life—"thanksliving." In this case, thanks-giving and praise are natural expressions of the soul. We do not give thanks because we have received (courtesy) or because we expect to receive (act of faith), but because we are expressing our true nature.

Thanksliving is evident when Paul and Silas were in prison as recorded in Acts 16:25–26. It was midnight, and they were praising and singing and giving thanks to God. Suddenly, the prison was shaken by an earthquake, and the doors of the prison were opened. Paul and Silas were free in Spirit, and the state of their souls was made mani-fest. Of this event, Charles Fillmore, cofounder of the Unity movement, surmised that spiritual forces act through exalted thoughts. Thanksgiving, when it is a natural expression of our souls, is a grand ex-ample of exalted thought. Spiritual forces act through these uplifted thoughts in ways that meet tangible needs.

Rejoice in these things and begin your journey to no-needs. This is the consciousness that reveals to us that we are in the kingdom, and all is well. Be aware of the human tendency to ask to have our needs fulfilled. Although this path is part of our rite of passage, it leads to limitation and lack. Let us ask, but let the desire of our heart be for God. When we seek Spirit, we find. When we knock on this door, it is opened unto us.

If words must be spoken, praise and give thanks. Join Paul and Silas in their prison cell, for from bondage comes freedom beyond compare. Lay up treasures in heaven. Sing, give thanks, and praise God, and then wait for the no-need state. It may appear empty, but it is the fountainhead of all good.

When human beings mired in lack look at the no-need state, they see a desert. How could this provide for their needs? When mystics look upon the same scene, the no-need state, they rejoice because they see a bountiful garden. Even in the winter the fields are white for harvest. Famine is no more. Contentment and fulfillment rule the land.

Key Ideas

1. Only the rich enter the kingdom of God.
2. When we know God, asking ceases.

3. When we are consciously one with God, we cannot want.
4. The no-need state manifests itself as our life experience. Through it, our earthly needs are met.
5. Thanksgiving prepares us for the kingdom of heaven.
6. Spiritual forces act through exalted thoughts. Thanksgiving and praise are examples of exalted thought.

Affirmation

The Lord is my shepherd; therefore, I cannot want.

Summary

I am rich when I have no needs.

Chapter
6

Prosperity's Demonstration

The Chest

Legend tells of a vagabond who begged for bread at a rich man's house. The wanderer was given food and a small, wooden chest. The rich man told the beggar that it would provide for his needs for the rest of his life, for it contained the riches of the universe.

Although he possessed the chest, the poor man was unable to open it. One day, hungry and disgusted with his life, the man determined that he would no longer look to others for his livelihood. With this thought, the box opened and within it was bread, water, and one gold coin. Each day thereafter the man looked to the box to provide for him, and he was supplied for seven days. On the eighth day, the box would not open.

Over the course of time, the man learned to look to God as his source, and the box opened and supplied his needs for seven years, but then it would not open again. Although the man was curious about the remaining treasures in the box, he was not concerned, for he had discovered his source.

Early one evening, he noticed a family before the charred ruins of their house. The wanderer, now a man rich in Spirit, desired to help them, and with this thought the box opened. Inside was a note with this inscription: *Give the family the box, for you have within you what you thought was in the box. Tell them that with its contents they can rebuild not only their house, but their lives.*

We mistakenly believe that prosperity is demonstrated when we receive—when money comes to us or we get a new job. This is not true. *Prosperity's demonstration is giving.* Our wise Creator has made giving a vital part of life's expression. We breathe in and receive oxygen, but it is just as important to exhale. The farmer wants to reap a bountiful harvest, but first he must sow the seeds.

Sowing is an act of faith. It is the farmer's demonstration. The harvest is nature's demonstration. The fruit on the vine and the grain on the ear are nature giving to the farmer and the world.

Giving does not depend upon what we have.

Studies of our society reveal that proportionally, the immensely wealthy are not the greatest givers in our country. They give only a small portion of what they have received. It is the middle income earner who is the greatest giver.

Giving depends upon our understanding of our spiritual nature. There once was a circuit-riding preacher who spoke one Wednesday evening at a small rural church. On this occasion, the man took his ten-year-old son with him. At the rear of the church was a box where the people placed their offering. As the preacher entered, he put a ten-dollar bill in the container. After the service, he was told that his honorarium was the money in the box. Inside was a single ten-dollar bill. As he and his son walked to their car, the young boy said, "I guess if you had put more in you would have gotten more out."

Is Giving Loss?

Although giving is essential to life, we are greatly challenged by the act. Even though the hand that gives is poised to receive, we are often reluctant to give. The reason is that we judge by appearances. We believe when we give, we incur a loss, for what we give we no longer have. To the human mind, nothing seems more true, but our wise Creator has designed a more compassionate universe.

The Truth is when we give, the one who receives is blessed, but the giver receives the greater blessing. The one who receives has something tangible to point to—the gift. The giver gains an expanded awareness of the way God's universe works and a consciousness that provides for every need.

At Christmas, have you ever witnessed a small child give a gift to a loved one? The little one stands before the person as he or she opens the present. The eyes of the child are aglow. This cheerful giver is filled with an expanded awareness of God's universe and at the least, it is joy. There is no sense of loss. The soul of the little one is full. In an instinctive way, the child experiences the essence of 2 Corinthians 9:7: "God loves a cheerful giver."

Rites of Passage of Giving

Spiritual understanding calls us to put aside our need to determine how to receive what we consider to be the blessings of life. Instead, it asks us to begin to investigate how to give, for giving is prosperity's demonstration.

There is a rite of passage that nearly every human being moves through as he or she learns to give. Each stage in giving tells us something about ourselves, and this understanding leads to the next step. None of the rites of passage is to be condemned, not even the first.

The first step seems to be no step; we do not give. Our belief in appearances, fear of tomorrow, and lack of understanding of the way the universe works close our hands. We cling to what we have even though it may be meager. Fear and insecurity grip the soul.

We do not give nor do we receive the riches of Spirit. Of course, our lack of giving is justified. We feel we don't have enough to give, or the people we would give to are not deserving: "They misuse other people's money, but they're not going to misuse mine." Excuses, but the real reason is fear.

We may fail to give, but deep within us we know giving is the key to life, so we begin. We give, but as little as possible and usually out of a sense of guilt. In a church setting, these are the individuals who give one dollar. Fear and insecurity are prevalent in their lives. They would like to give more, they say, but they are barely making ends meet. They don't see how they can do it. For them, giving must be out of abundance. When they win the lottery, they have big plans to become benefactors of the common good.

Fear reigns in the lives of these people, but another factor is at work. The real issue is values. For instance, on Saturday night these individuals may enjoy an evening of entertainment, a meal at a good restaurant and a movie. The night out could cost from twenty to fifty dollars or even more. It may even be memorable, but in many instances, it is quickly forgotten.

The next morning these people attend a worship service. Principles are shared that apply to their daily lives, or they may have an experience which touches their souls deeply. When the opportunity to give arrives, a dollar is given.

This is not a matter of making ends meet. The issue is values. Fine food and entertainment are more valuable than spiritual principles and life-changing experiences. Such people do not need to give more. They need to examine their values.

Mark 12:41–44 tells the tale of someone who examined her values. "And he sat down opposite the treasury, and watched the multitude putting money into the treasury. Many rich people put in large sums. And a poor widow came, and put in two copper coins, which make a penny. And he called his disciples to him, and said to them, 'Truly, I say to you, this poor widow has put in more than all those who are contributing to the treasury. For they all contributed out of their abundance; but she out of her poverty has put in everything she had, her whole living.'"

I speculate about this woman. She is one of the Bible characters I wish I knew. It would be interesting to know the circumstances of her life prior to her day at the treasury. Likewise, I would like to know what happened to her after she gave at the temple. As Jesus said, she put in her whole living.

She must have valued her spirituality above all else. You can be assured that she broke through into the kingdom of God and found a security transcending human circumstance.

The third step in the unfoldment of a giving consciousness is giving out of a sense of duty. We give because we believe we should. Perhaps someone causes us to consider our values, so we give. We may even give generously, but there is no joy.

True joy comes when we do not give because we should, but so we can come alive. Many years ago when my family was on vacation, we were browsing in a department store and I was looking at sports equipment. There was a young boy, perhaps ten or eleven years old, buying a soccer ball. He must have saved his money, for he was taking crumpled dollar bills and coins from every pocket in his pants. The clerk counted the money, and the boy was less than a dollar short. He was downcast. The price of the ball must have increased from the time he first priced it or perhaps he forgot to include tax.

I reached into my pocket and took out a dollar and gave it to the clerk. She rang up the sale and asked me if I wanted the change. I said, "No, give it to the boy," and continued my browsing. As the boy ran out of the store, he said to me, "Thanks," and

he was gone. For me, the boy was an angel. I gave
only a dollar, but after he left I was trembling. The joy
of giving moved me at the core of my being. I learned
a powerful lesson. I have always wondered about the
young lad. Was it two human beings who came together briefly, or was he a gift from God to me? When
we give out of duty, we do not tremble with joy.

The fourth rite of passage is giving to get. This
may be based on the misconception that money is
power or a way to wield control. We give to get a
"payoff." Obviously, we must feel a certain degree
of powerlessness to think and behave in this way.

For other people, giving to get is based upon spiritual principle, "It is more blessed to give than to
receive" (Acts 20:35). They look to the farmers and
say, "As we sow, so shall we reap." Giving begins,
but a payoff is demanded. Teachers may say that
God wants us to prosper and have whatever we
want. I say God has given us what we need; let us
become aware of it.

Giving is not prosperity's first demonstration. It
is the only demonstration. Giving allows us to become
aware of the Presence. It is not a way to get things
or to have our earthly wants and needs fulfilled.

When we give so we can receive, we may seem
to prosper for a time. We can even become addicted
to this way of life. We establish a goal, and it is fulfilled. We look again at our life and determine what
it is that we do not have, and another goal comes

into being. The tragedy is that a spiritual being is now "sowing to the flesh." The seed that is harvested as an increased awareness of the Presence is not even sown. When we give to receive, we receive little. Many people even discover that after a time, it doesn't work any more. When this occurs or a void fills the soul, it is definitely time for another way.

Finally, the breakthrough occurs. *We give because it is our nature.* Nothing is more natural than to give. Children may fight over their toys, but they are most alive when they give. To give is to be alive—to express what we truly are. To take, withhold, hoard, or give to get is to feel less than alive and less than who we are.

Eventually, we give because it is our nature. When people give you an opportunity to give, they are giving you a great blessing. It is an opportunity to express your true nature. Don't miss it.

God First

Let us assume you have the possibility of receiving a large amount of money. You are told that you must compile a list of the first five things you would do with the gift and that your list will determine if you receive the funds. You have forty days to determine what you will do. (Hint: The first thing you must do with the money is the same whether the gift is one dollar or one million dollars).

Perhaps you will see the first thing you must do with your gift on a car bumper sticker—"If you love Jesus, tithe; anyone can honk." Tithing makes prosperity's demonstration a way of life; however, humanity has a narrow view of tithing. Most people believe it is giving 10 percent of their income to a church or spiritually based institution. In the Old Testament, there are numerous references to tithing, and we will examine several of them. However, when tithing came into being there was no church. In fact, the financial system was based on barter, not money.

The confusion about tithing increases when we discover that Jesus did not talk about it. There are only two references to tithing in The Gospels, and both times Jesus is speaking to the religious leaders who tithe, but who have forgotten the heart of the spiritual practice.

But Jesus did teach tithing. In fact, it was the heart of his ministry, but he did not teach tithing as it is generally taught today—giving 10 percent of one's income to the church.

From the mystical standpoint, tithing is a consciousness of God first. When something wonderful happens in our lives and our first thought is "Thank you, God," we have tithed, for we know our source and have placed God first. When a challenging event occurs and our first response is, "Where's the good in this?" we are tithing. There are numerous ways we express our attitude of God first. When the most important time of our day is our prayer time, we are tithing. Likewise, we can put God first in our financial affairs.

As we continue to explore tithing, let us remember that primarily it is an attitude of God first. When we live life in this way, we are blessed immensely. This is why people who tithe prosper. It is not because of the money they give, but because they put Spirit first in their lives in numerous ways. We can determine if God is first in our lives by looking at what we do with our time and money.

When God is first, we give time to knowing God and serving Spirit by helping others and by being involved in the uplifting of the consciousness of our planet. We pray; we meditate; we study Truth. To give 10 percent of our time to these endeavors is just, for God is our creator and sustainer.

Giving 10 percent of our income to support the unfoldment of spirituality on our planet seems fair. God is our source. All that we have comes from this storehouse. When we know this, God is first, and we act out of this spiritual realization. It is one thing to know it intellectually; it is another to live our lives based upon this Truth and to do the work that Spirit guides us to do. "So faith by itself, if it has no works, is dead" (Jas. 2:17).

Logically, 10 percent may seem just to you, also, but if you have never tithed before, this may seem too much. If this is the case, start at 1 percent of your income. It can be before or after taxes. It doesn't matter—just begin. Then each month increase your giving until you reach 10 percent. As you progress monthly, look for the "wall." At some point, you will conclude: "I cannot do this. It will bring financial ruin. The ends will not meet if I tithe." This is the wall tithers face.

Consider that the novice tither is actually saying: "I cannot put God first. Putting God first will bring financial ruin. The ends will not meet if I put God first." How untrue the statements become when we realize that tithing is putting God first. No one has ever put God first and failed.

Only good comes from putting Spirit first. Every person stands before the wall. As we recommit to putting Spirit first, the wall becomes a bridge to a deeper spiritual life and more prosperous and secure living.

The First Tither

Abram, who became Abraham, was the first tither. The fourteenth chapter of Genesis records his story. Abram rescued his kinsman Lot who had been taken captive. On the way home, Melchizedek, a priest, blessed Abram: "Blessed be Abram by God Most High, maker of heaven and earth." Abram responded by giving a tenth of everything to Melchizedek.

This event tells us where we give our tithe—to

the avenue through which we receive a spiritual blessing. It could be a person, an institution, or a church. There are many possibilities. It is important that we remain sensitive to the blessings of Spirit and the channels through which they come. Spirit is the source, but the Infinite is made manifest through many avenues. By tithing to the channels of our spiritual good, we create a circulation that blesses others and supports God's work upon this planet.

God's Challenge

In Malachi 3:10, God challenged humanity. "Bring the full tithes into the storehouse, that there may be food in my house; and thereby put me to the test, says the Lord of hosts, if I will not open the windows of heaven for you and pour down for you an overflowing blessing." This challenge was issued because the people were not putting God first.

In ancient times, the people did not tithe by giving money. They tithed by giving the fruits of their labor, good seed from the fields, and unblemished lambs which were sacrificed. This seems primitive to us, but this was their way of giving. However, the people to whom Malachi spoke were no longer putting God first, for the lambs they sacrificed were deformed or diseased. The seeds they gave were damaged and unlikely to produce a bountiful harvest. Basically, the people put themselves first rather than God. Outwardly they tithed, but inwardly fear of tomorrow ruled their actions.

The scripture in Malachi tells us that a principle is at work. Our actions are not as important as our attitude. Let us put God first, not so we can receive a great blessing, but because our life not only began in God, but continues to be born anew each day in Spirit. We have no lambs to sacrifice, but we have time, attention, and money to give. God deserves more than what remains after we have had our fill of earthly life. Put God first, not so you can be blessed, but because being a blessing is your way of life.

Key Ideas

1. Prosperity's demonstration is giving.
2. Giving does not depend upon what we have. Giving depends upon our understanding of our spiritual nature and our values.
3. Giving allows us to become aware of the Presence.
4. The giver gains an expanded awareness of the way God's universe works and a consciousness that provides for every need.
5. Rites of passage of giving:
    • We do not give.
    • We give out of a sense of guilt.

- We give out of a sense of duty.
- We give in order to receive.
- We give because it is our nature.
6. Tithing is putting God first.
7. Tithing makes prosperity's demonstration a way of life.

Affirmation

I give because it is my nature to give.

Summary

Giving is prosperity's demonstration.

CHAPTER
7

And the Quail Came

The spiritual realm is mysterious and unknown to most of humankind. We sense its power, but only a few God-centered individuals have tapped the kingdom and allowed its power to give rise to miracles and wonders. These saintly ones encourage us to do likewise, but their demands of humility, stillness, and nonresistance seem impractical in today's world. Yet the power of the Presence has been made manifest.

We wish it could be for us as it was for the Hebrews as they wandered in the wilderness. They were without food, and in the morning manna was on the ground. When they longed for meat, the quail came. We now know that God is our source, and a consciousness of God is our supply, but for many of us, manifestation is what we want. In the morning, we look for manna on the ground and later in the day to the sky for the coming of the quail.

Manifestation may preoccupy us, but we must not make a god of it, for we cannot "serve God and mammon" (Mt. 6:24). Mammon is manifestation, but when life is lived from a divine center, manifestation is none of our business. It is a shower of blessing that rains upon us because we seek the kingdom and desire to know God.

We seek the kingdom, but it is helpful to learn the path that begins with God and ends as a blessing in our lives. Manifestation, for instance a new job or an unexpected sum of money, is the initial reason people learn the principles of prosperity. They do not want God; they want to prosper. The premise is that if they work in harmony with the principles, they will be blessed. This is the path we all trod, and it is not to be condemned, but we cannot find joy by continuously vacillating between serving God and manifestation.

From the Kingdom to Our Daily Lives

The Presence is pure Silence, for God is not a thought, feeling, or image. When we enter the kingdom, the human faculties of thinking, feeling, and imagination are asleep. Remember the commandment: "You shall have no other gods before me. You shall not make for yourself a graven image" (Ex. 20:3–4). A thought, feeling, or image is just as much a graven image as a stone idol. Yet the wonder of God's universe is that there is movement from the Silence into our daily lives.

First, there is Silence, a state of consciousness without thought, feeling, or image. This divine silence then begins its journey into manifestation. A thought, feeling, or image may enter our minds. Ideas may come to us.

Spirit has Its role, and we have ours. A consciousness of the Source first manifests Itself as a feeling of well-being and security. At this point, nothing has changed in our outer world, but our inner world is changing. The quail are coming; manifestation is on its way. When this occurs, it is important to keep our focus on God. We derail the process when we shift our attention to what is being made manifest. We may even select what we think must come into being.

There are more gifts to be received in the secret place within our souls. After the feeling of well-being and security—ideas, thoughts, or images may come to us. These intangible, highly private gifts of Spirit serve as a bridge from the kingdom of God to our daily lives.

Our role is to be receptive to ideas and to act upon them. Every new company, every new product was once an idea in the mind of a human being.

It was a gift and a bridge which allowed the power that God is to come into being.

In the early part of the twentieth century, a business person received a prospering idea. In those times, laundries put a piece of cardboard in men's shirts to keep them wrinkle-free. The shirts came to the customer with the cardboard insert. The idea was to put advertisements on the insert, so when people removed the cardboard they would see the advertisement. Utilizing this practice, a prosperous business began. Next another idea came—put a game for children on the back of the cardboard so the advertisement would not be immediately tossed aside but would remain in the house to be seen. Prosperity begins as an idea that requires not only receptive minds, but action and hard work.

Look for the Quail

People have prospered in every kind of economic climate. This is because our supply, a consciousness of God, is unaffected by economic conditions. It is a law of life that spiritual awareness must manifest itself. One of the first manifestations is ideas. They are freeing and limitless like the birds of the air. Perhaps this is why Jesus said, "The kingdom of heaven is like a grain of mustard seed which a man took and sowed in his field; it is the smallest of all seeds, but when it has grown it is the greatest of shrubs and becomes a tree, so that the birds of the air come and make nests in its branches" (Mt. 13:31–32). The kingdom, our awareness of God, is like a seed because it grows. Eventually, it becomes like a great shrub that attracts the birds of the air or ideas that become a blessing.

The people of Jesus' time considered heaven to be in the sky. This is why birds are interpreted to be ideas, for they soar above the Earth. They are closest to the "heaven" of ancient times. Divine ideas are the link between the Silence and our daily lives. Remember, the ravens fed the prophet. I am sure in the infinite realm of God's presence, ravens could literally feed a spiritually aware person, but it is also true that ideas have lifted many a person to new heights, nourished the soul, and prospered him or her.

It is important to be sensitive to ideas; it is also vital to watch for opportunities. Our awareness of God often manifests itself in this way. An opportunity comes, and as we act upon it, we prosper. Opportunities are one step closer to the kingdom. First, there is Silence, then the sense of the Presence experienced as a feeling of security or peace. Next an idea may come as a thought or image, or we may be given an opportunity. In this instance, it is important that we recognize the gift we have been given: perhaps someone may offer us a new job, or we may receive an invitation to attend a lecture that changes our life. The possibilities are infinite.

Finally, we must act. Deposits will most likely not be made in our checking account. We must invest in the Infinite by acting upon the guidance, ideas, and opportunities we receive.

This is the message recorded in Matthew 25:14–30. As a rich man prepared to go on a journey, he called three of his servants to him. To one he gave five talents. (A talent was fifteen years' wages for a laborer.) To the second servant, he gave two talents and to the third, one talent—"each according to his ability." The first two servants doubled their talents. The third servant was afraid of losing what he had, so he buried it.

When the master returned and learned what they had done with their talents, he praised the first two servants but admonished the third. The first two people opened their minds and became receptive to ideas, and they prospered. The third worker allowed fear to close his mind, and he lost what he had. "So take the talent from him, and give it to him who has the ten talents. For to every one who has will more be given, and he will have abundance; but from him who has not, even what he has will be taken away."

We are not servants of a rich man, but life gives us opportunities to open our minds to ideas. In this way, the kingdom is made manifest in our lives. The quail came for the Hebrews, but I can assure you that first there was a consciousness of God.

There are numerous examples of prosperity demonstrations in the Bible—the manna and quail of the Hebrews, Jesus' feeding of the 5000, Elisha's multiplication of the oil, etc., but the demonstration is not the issue. Remember, we do not serve mammon. The issue is the consciousness that could manifest itself in these ways. This is worthy of our attention.

A consciousness of God is continuously manifesting itself in our lives, but we often fail to see the manna on the ground and the quail in the air. We think our prosperity comes in the form of our paychecks or interests and dividends. In most people's lives, there are numerous other expressions of our awareness of our source. When a friend takes us out to dinner, this is a manifestation of our consciousness and a prosperity demonstration for our friend. When our neighbor shares vegetables from his garden, we are blessed. *For a period of seven days, make a record of these kinds of instances, and you will discover blessings which you have overlooked for years.* The avenues through which you are blessed are numerous, for even as you read these words, the quail are coming.

Key Ideas

1. We cannot serve God and mammon.
2. A consciousness of our source first manifests itself as a feeling of well-being and security.

3.   Next may come thoughts, feelings, or images.
4.   Ideas are a prime manifestation of the Silence.
5.   Ideas are a bridge between the kingdom and our daily lives.
6.   We must act upon the ideas we receive and recognize the opportunities presented to us.

Affirmation

Manifestation is none of my business.

Summary

Manifestation begins in the Silence.

SECTION TWO

Put Them to the Test

I love the idea of an experiment. I propose that we put to the test the principles outlined in the first section of this book. Let it be as it was in the days of Malachi, "Put me to the test, says the Lord of hosts, if I will not open the windows of heaven for you and pour down for you an overflowing blessing" (Mal. 3:10). If we answer this challenge, then we will know from experience whether the so-called truths are true. If they cannot be lived in the home, if they cannot guide us in our business dealings, if a church cannot prosper by declaring God as its Source, and if the world cannot be a better place through the application of these "truths," then they must be discarded, and we must find another way.

There is too much at stake for us not to accept this challenge, and the world's needs are too great for us to pursue any avenue that will not bring us to an awareness of our source. For a time, let us put aside the idea of solving the world's problems of famine and despair and begin with our own households.

CHAPTER
8

Prosperity in the Home

Prosperity in the home is not simply a matter of money, and yet how many of us have thought we didn't have any problems that a million dollars wouldn't solve? Beneath our desire for money, stronger issues are at work that money cannot buy—security, self-worth, and ultimately the discovery of who we are and why we are here.

The infinite Source is within us; therefore, nothing needs to be added to us. A way must be found so the Fountainhead, the wellspring of living water, can find its way from the dark depths of our earthly desire into the light where it can quench our greater thirst for meaning, security, and discovery.

This is paramount, for most of us begin our adult lives with the hope that we will prosper and with the aspiration that we will enjoy the good life. Then the years march on. We allow circumstances to dash our dreams. We struggle to make ends meet or fear the future. Past unwise decisions seem to limit our todays and our tomorrows.

In the home where the ends do not meet, the ends unravel. Tension builds. We question not only our financial worth, but our self-worth. We suffer; we struggle; we feel insecure. There is no boldness in us. Usually relationships are strained. There is much pain because we do not know our source and the true nature of supply. It may be that all we have is hope and the willingness to put to the test not only prosperity principles, but a new way of living. These two, hope and willingness, are a good beginning.

The family has its needs, but we know they are not the real issue. The question is, Will a consciousness of God dawn in us? This is the work of all members of the family. Children need to know their source and the true nature of supply just as much as adults. Adults tend to look to their employment as their source and money as supply. Children tend to look to their parents as the source. Both are mistaken.

A Prosperity Plan for the Home

No amount of planning can ensure that any member of the family will awaken spiritually and become rich in Spirit. The revelation is an act of grace and is God's work; however, we have our work to do. None of the steps about to be outlined can create the breakthrough, but they can stir our current consciousness and open us to God's grace.

Steps and Suggestions

One of our primary problems is allowing thoughts of lack to dominate our thinking. We support such thoughts, but they do not support our dreams. Thinking lack is one of the pennies of Chapter 3. Remember the principle: "For to every one who has will more be given, and he will have abundance; but from him who has not, even what he has will be taken away" (Mt. 25:29). The have-not consciousness produces more lack, for we continue to lose what we have. This kind of thinking must cease, but it is easier said than done.

Our first step is thanksgiving, for when we are thankful, positive thoughts begin to dominate our thinking. *My suggestion is that the family gather together and make a list of all the things for which they are thankful.* The list may begin with earthly things, but don't forget to include one another and the intangible qualities of life that endure.

The practice of thankfulness turns our thinking from what we do not have (the have-not consciousness) to what we have. Remember, "to every one who has will more be given," and the first gift is an awareness of God. This is our supply, and it will eventually provide for our earthly needs.

My second suggestion is that whenever you receive a check made out to you, endorse it as you always do and then write below your signature the word Blessings. This simple act is a tangible way of saying thank-you, for through our banking system, the canceled check returns to the one who issued it. The important point is not that the check returns, but our attitude when we receive a blessing. A prosperous person does not blindly move through life. He or she is aware of blessings received. They are the person's consciousness manifesting itself. Therefore, there is a connectedness between a check received and the infinite supply. This understanding yields thankfulness.

A family may be plagued by negative thinking, but fear of the future is likewise limiting. Those who fear tomorrow hoard their belongings. Let us look at our closets and storage areas. Do we really need all that stuff? Some, it is said, has sentimental value. If this is true, why are these valuable artifacts that are so much a part of our lives stored in the attic and other out-of-the-way places? One would assume that something so precious would be displayed for us and others to see, or that it would be used each day. Sometimes we say, "I may need that one day." Perhaps we will, but how will we find it since we have no inventory of the items that are in the attic, the back of the closet, or in the basement? In many instances, we have forgotten what we have.

The truth is we hoard because we feel insecure, believe in a limited supply, and fear what tomorrow may bring. We accumulate stuff because we mistakenly think it makes us secure, but hoarding actually contributes to our sense of limitation and feelings of insecurity.

Exodus 16:13–30 illustrates what happens when we hoard. After the Hebrews escaped from Egypt, manna fed them while they wandered in the wilderness. It was their daily bread—a gift of God that sustained them for years as they meandered toward the promised land. God's guidance concerning the manna was clear. Each family was to gather what it needed for one day. Only on the day before the Sabbath were the Hebrews to gather twice as much manna as usual. This cache of daily bread ensured the holy day would be a day of rest.

At first, the people did not heed God's direction. Their fear of tomorrow caused them to gather more than they needed. When they awoke, the hoarded manna was foul and filled with worms. This happens when we believe in a limited supply and fear tomorrow. Our fear and thoughts of lack spoil what we have. It may be our belongings or our state of mind, but there is spoilage.

Remember, God is our source, and a conscious-ness of God is our supply. It is like the manna—available each day. No one can hoard it. There is no need to: an awareness of God is available each moment of each day.

It is suggested that the family, whether it is one or many people, "purge" the home. Go through the closets, drawers, attic, basement, and storage areas to locate items that are no longer in use. A good rule of thumb is if an item has not been used in a full season (like a winter coat), then it is time to let it go. Give your items away or have a garage sale.

Letting go is important. The Great Salt Lake in Utah and the Dead Sea between Jordan and Israel are examples of what happens when we have no outlet. These are lifeless bodies of water because they hoard the water that enters their basins. Purging our houses opens our souls to greater security and helps us learn the lesson that the manna taught the Hebrews. Surely, the daily bread was a blessing to their earthly lives, but the greater blessing was their understanding of their source.

Paying Our Bills

When we are rich in Spirit, we pay our bills with joy. When we are poor, if we pay our bills, we often do so begrudgingly. The power company has supplied us with electricity for a month, allowing us to live in relative comfort and to do things associated with modern living, but we resent having to pay the bill. We have so many current needs, and what about tomorrow? We reluctantly mail the payment but wish we could use the money for another purpose. This attitude and behavior are signs of a consciousness of lack, a belief in a limited supply and fear of tomorrow.

Many people have begun to pay their bills in a different way. In the lower left-hand corner of their checks where "For" is imprinted or on the bills they return with payment, they write, "Blessings" or "Thank You, God." They have received a service, so they give thanks. This does three things. It acknowledges God as the Source, expresses joy rather than resentment when paying bills, and establishes a giving state of mind. These are chief ingredients in the heart of a prosperous person. The rich one knows the importance of attitude when dealing with money. When resentment and reluctance are replaced by a desire to bless, the great blessing that only God can give is rising from the fountainhead within us.

Keeping Up With the Joneses

Who are the Joneses, and how did they get so prosperous? Why do we envy and dislike them, bemoan their wealth, and question how they obtained it? On the surface, envy is about the Joneses, but because envy is a feeling *we have* when we begrudge someone the blessings of his or her life, envy actually masks beliefs we hold about ourselves.

It appears that we want what the other person has, but the truth is we do not believe we have the ability to experience life in a similar way. Basically, envy is a feeling which hides a deep, often unconscious belief that we cannot become aware of our source. This is a lie.

Infinite states of consciousness are available to us. When we open ourselves to a new awareness, we will not resent what others have or try to "keep up with the Joneses." We will rejoice with them. Then we will give our attention to the depths of our souls and let an awareness of God's unlimited supply sweep over us. In this way, we gain not the possessions of another or even duplicate what another has acquired. Instead, we experience another dimension of the kingdom of God. This is of greater value than any earthly thing.

Learning to Save

Financial planners tell us that we should have six months of our income in a savings account to prepare us for the unfortunate circumstance of loss of our job or other income. It would be nice. It makes logical sense, but what happens after the six months if we do not have another job? To what savings account will we turn?

It is good to save our money, but not for a future setback. Even if we are able to heed the advice of financial planners, we are not secure. Our treasure is in heaven, and this is where we must build our reserves.

This does not mean we do not save money or that each day we live on a financial precipice. We may save a portion of our income, but not for an emergency. *Instead, let us create an opportunity fund. Many people actually label their account in this way.* It may be used for house repairs, as a down payment on another house, a long-awaited vacation, education for the children, or a special gift for a friend, worthy organization, or cause.

Please realize that opening an opportunity fund or doing the other things which have been suggested or which will be suggested will not make you prosperous and secure. This is God's work, for a spiritual awakening is required. We cannot force this experience, but the suggested activities help to prepare the soul for its breakthrough.

Riches Without Possessions

Some of the blocks to prosperity are subtle. On the surface, prosperity is one of the easiest principles of Truth to prove, but as the soul unfolds, refinements are required. For instance, at first the woodcarver chips away coarse pieces of wood, and the form seen in the mind begins to emerge. However, eventually sandpaper is used so minute fragments of wood can be removed.

In the early stages of our prosperity development, we think we are making progress because our income increases or because we add new possessions to the household. As the years of growth come and go, we see these events in another way.

Eventually, we discover that we must drop from our consciousness the idea of possession. "The earth is the Lord's and the fulness thereof, the world and those who dwell therein" (Ps. 24:1). A belief in possession is a block to prosperity. This would not be true if we were solely human beings. It is obvious that human beings possess many things. We even have deeds, mortgages, bills of sale to prove a thing is ours. This belief in possessions must find its proper place.

Through the practice of the Jubilee Year explained in Chapter 3, the Hebrews attempted to put aside the idea of possession by returning land to the previous owner after 50 years.

The idea of possession reinforces the belief that we are exclusively human beings, but we are much more. We are spiritual beings possessing nothing and having no need to possess anything. What earthly thing does a spiritual being need? Does a spiritual being need an automobile for transportation or a house for shelter?

A spiritual being needs a consciousness of Truth. This is more than shelter; it is a state in which to dwell. It is more than transportation; it moves us deep into the kingdom of God. Of course, these words express the absolute Truth, but they must not be forgotten. Let there be balance between the Truth of our being and our human existence. In this way, we render unto Caesar what is Caesar's and unto God what is God's.

We may own a home and the clothes we wear, and we may have paid off the note on the automobile, but let there be no possessions. Is this possible? Yes, for possession is a state of mind. Just as a move to another city is encumbered by many possessions, so a possessive state of mind makes it difficult for us to release what we think makes us rich and secure. However, when we let go of the idea of possession, we find a greater treasure in heaven.

The 80 Percent Plan

The prosperous family tithes; it puts God first in all areas of life, including finances. The truth is we cannot clutch money as if it were our savior and truly prosper. By tithing and putting God first, we find that not only are our needs met but we become rich in Spirit. The tithe can be from either the gross or net pay that we receive, but it must be before expenses. If it is not, God is not first, we are. In fact, it is best when the first funds disbursed from each paycheck are our tithe.

As I said earlier, 10 percent of our income may seem like too much. If this is the case, let us start with 1 percent and increase our giving each month until we reach 11 percent of our income. We move beyond 10 percent because tithing is a consciousness of God first rather than an act of giving. The essence of any spiritual principle lies in consciousness rather than what we do. However, consciousness must manifest itself in actions and daily living. What we do must be consistent with what we say we believe.

Some might say, then why not give at a rate of 5 percent or 1 percent? Is the percentage important in declaring God first? Attitude is more important than the amount we give, but the issue is values and equity. Is 1 percent a fair and just gift when we consider what God gives us? Through the ages, those who pondered such things concluded that sharing 10 percent of all which we have is a fair contribution to Spirit's work upon the planet.

The Next Step

The next step of the 80 percent plan is to put 9 percent of our income in an opportunity fund.

This is our savings, not for a rainy day, but for some unexpected opportunity. It may be something that blesses our family, or it may bless others.

Years ago a strange and wonderful thing happened to us. A young boy was going door-to-door selling positive children's music (records) on a love offering basis. There was no set price; we could give what we wanted to give. Nancy and I viewed this as a great opportunity, and we gave all we could give. Sometimes I wonder if the boy was not an angel giving us the opportunity to give.

Adjust Your Lifestyle

In the 80 percent plan, we first give 11 percent of our income to support the unfoldment of God's work on the planet. Next, we set aside 9 percent of our income for ourselves and some opportunity that will be ours at a future time.

Living on the remaining 80 percent of our income may seem difficult if not impossible. We declare, "It takes every cent I have to make ends meet." My answer is: "Is this the way you want to continue to live your life? There is another way."

There is an infinite supply in the midst of us. Our giving and other practices outlined in this book help open the gateway of our souls, so the "imprisoned splendor" can escape and become a great blessing to us and the world.

The most prosperous people in the world do not use their money only for themselves. They understand their obligation to be servants of the many. We may not be one of these benevolent supporters of humanity, but we can begin this journey with the plan outlined in this chapter.

Our supply is our growing awareness of God. With it, security grows too. At first we will feel better, but nothing will change. However, if we are open, eventually our consciousness of God will manifest itself as our life.

Begin the process of adjusting your lifestyle, so you can live the 80 percent plan. Eighty percent of your income is to be used for your immediate needs. Nine percent rests in the opportunity fund for some future use that may bless your family and others. And 11 percent of all that you have received is dedicated to the unfoldment of truth upon this planet.

Conclusion

Prosperity in the home, like prosperity in business or in a religious setting, is an opportunity to experience God as Source. Individuals involved in consciousness-raising are often greatly challenged when they try to put into practice the ideas and principles that excite their minds. It is invigorating to talk about Truth, but the talk is often a way of avoiding daily life—a difficult thing to avoid!

The ongoing struggle is the practical application of Truth. Today can be a new beginning. We are aware of spiritual truths that enable us to be true to the high, mystical calling to know God. We have also been given ideas to balance the heavenly with earthly action. Let us begin today, and the excitement that fills our minds will fill our lives.

Key Ideas

1. Prosperity in the home is not simply a matter of money.
2. One of our prosperity problems is thinking lack.
3. When we are thankful, we allow positive thoughts to dominate our minds.
4. Another prosperity problem is fear. Fear causes us to hoard.
5. A consciousness of God is our daily bread. There is no need to hoard it.
6. A consciousness of God cannot be limited and is available to everyone.
7. A belief in possession is a block to prosperity.

A Prosperity Plan

1. Ask the members of your family to make a list of all the things for which they are thankful.
2. Whenever you receive a check, endorse it, and

then below your name, write the word *Bless-ings*.
3. Stop hoarding by purging your home.
4. Establish the 80 percent plan by living on 80 percent of your income.
5. Put God first by tithing 11 percent of your income.
6. Set aside 9 percent of your income in an opportunity fund.

Affirmation

Today I take steps that prepare me for a spiritual awakening.

Summary

I put into practice the spiritual truths that I have learned.

Chapter
9

Business Practices in the 21st Century

Business or Busyness, Which?

The business world and the kingdom of God are not far from one another. Spiritual principles work whether they are practiced in our home, in a church, at work, or in a global economy. They cannot be true and effective in one area of life and not in another.

The world needs courageous people who will hold to these principles and not succumb to the adage that the "end justifies the means." Appearances declare that it is a dog-eat-dog world and that the Golden Rule is an invitation to failure. These are the beliefs of those who practice busyness.

A call is now going out for a new kind of innovative business leader and worker. The search is on for spiritual entrepreneurs who will enter into partnership with God. These executives and their associates will be subject to local, national, and world economic conditions, but they will rise above them. They will put to rest the false belief that there is God's business and then there is business in the world. An ancient promise will be fulfilled. "And every work that he undertook in the service of the house of God and in accordance with the law and the commandments, seeking his God, he did with all his heart, and prospered" (2 Chr. 31:21).

To Toil and Spin?

"Consider the lilies of the field, how they grow; they neither toil nor spin; yet I tell you, even Solomon in all his glory was not arrayed like one of these" (Mt. 6:28–29). We have a choice. We can toil and spin and succeed in exhaustion as we pursue our careers, or we can be like the lilies of the field and succeed in being true to our nature. Ulcers, hypertension, alcoholism, drug abuse, heart disease, and broken families are testimonies to the disorientation that comes from spinning. Peace, prosperity, and purpose come to those true to what they are.

Toiling results in burnout. Spinning causes us to lose our way. We go to work, but life is without meaning. The lily is a thing of beauty because it is true to its nature. It does not try to be something it is not or to live contrary to the God-ordained principles that govern its growth.

We, too, are destined to be fruitful and give expression to the beauty that is within us, so first let us be true to our nature. When we make money and career the reason for being, we have forgotten what we are. Toiling and spinning have begun. "For what does it profit a man if he gains the whole world and loses or forfeits himself?" (Lk. 9:25)

When a company focuses upon the bottom line at the expense of service, it toils and spins. When shareholders are more highly valued than those the company serves or the workers who do the work, deterioration is underway and exhaustion is near. For a time, the company may appear successful, but even success will be a struggle. Eventually, those who live life in this way lose themselves.

In Partnership With God

Wouldn't it be wonderful to be in partnership with God? Imagine the guidance and resources available to do the work that the company was founded to do. What if we did not have to be executives in the business to be a partner? What if the partnership could begin the first day of employment?

Oneness with Spirit is as much the destiny of a construction worker, teacher, salesperson, and engineer as it is the destiny of a spiritual leader. All aspects of earthly experience, including our career, can be a cup overflowing with peace and joy. Our professional life can be one more place where we experience life to the fullest.

Careers and businesses usually begin with innocence and idealism. We want to succeed. We are going to give our all for the good of the company, and in the process, we are going to prosper. Day-to-day life often dashes this age of innocence. Idealism is sometimes replaced by cynicism. Dreams of success and prosperity are met by failure and what we consider to be a mediocre lifestyle. We are not in partnership with God. In fact, we may be at odds with our supervisor or even our coworkers.

How easy it is to try to form a partnership with the god of the bottom line or financial success. After all, if the company doesn't prosper, it cannot exist, and if it does not exist, how will it serve? If we don't prosper, how will we provide for our families or do the things we feel will bring us happiness?

This is a critical time in the life of a company or in a career. Idealism and innocence are dying. It is time to ask ourselves what we will gain if we "succeed" but lose ourselves. One of the great gifts a spiritual entrepreneur gives the world is idealism. Those with the highest ideals make the greatest contribution to the unfoldment of humanity. No matter how life batters us, we can maintain our innocence by holding to principles and values that yield not only a successful career, but a meaningful life.

The issue is not so much our profession as it is living the ideals. Just as it is with all aspects of earthly experience, our career is an outpicturing of our most heartfelt beliefs and values. If this is not true, we may succeed in busyness but fail in life. Our career may seem to make sense, but life will be without meaning. We may gain much in an earthly sense but lose ourselves.

The Values of the 21st Century Business Leader

Every circle has a center around which the circumference forms. Every business has a leader or group of people who serve as the center of the circle. Success begins here. Actually, the *values* of the chief executive officer or board of directors determine the success of the business. Ideally, these values are not company policies; they are the fundamental building blocks of a life of oneness with God. They are evident when there is a partnership with Spirit.

Value #1

"Where there is no vision, the people perish" (Prov. 29:18 KJV). If we venture into the center of the circle, we will find a vision. A vision or reason for being is a key element of a successful spiritual enterprise and individual career. A vision is something to which people can give their lives. It engages a person's unique talents and calls forth creativity. A vision helps people discover their place in the world and contributes to an individual's understanding of why he or she is here. It is a reason for being other than making money and supporting one's self or family. A vision turns existence into a meaningful life.

Years ago Sir Christopher Wren, a famous architect and builder, was walking through a construction site. He asked one worker what he was doing. The man said that he was making a shilling a day. This man was working for money. A second worker was asked the same question. He said that he was building a wall. This man's vision was limited to his task. Sir Christopher Wren asked a third worker what he was doing. The man stood up not knowing to whom he was talking and proudly answered, "I am helping Sir Christopher Wren build the greatest cathedral in the world."

This is vision. It places the newest worker or the person at the lowest salary grade level in the company in the center of the circle with the chief executive officer and board of directors.

Value #2

"The Son of man came not to be served but to serve" (Mt. 20:28). In a partnership with God, none of the values stands alone. Vision is the center of the circle, but when we draw near to it, we discover that its name is service. *Service* is the seed that bears fruit as a successful enterprise, career, and life.

It has been said, find a need and fill it. Every business begins with an idea. Ideas by their nature are not of this world, but they can assume an earthly form. In many instances, they help humankind fulfill its needs. These needs range from food, clothing, and communication to cosmetics, entertainment, and medical needs.

America with its capitalistic system is called the land of opportunity. Millions of immigrants come here in search of a better life. May they discover that America is foremost a place where the individual is given an opportunity to serve others and to help them fulfill their needs. May they find that capitalism is not a system in which to build capital, but a way of life in which our capital aim is to serve others.

When we are in partnership with God, we are here not to be served but to serve. Our reason for being is greater than our existence. As we perform our tasks, let us be sensitive to the tendency for this ideal to become lost in busyness.

A successful company experiences a steady flow of ideas that serves the needs of others. Service is its vision, its reason for being, so the ideas come one after another. There is no resting on last year's innovation. A vision of service demands ever-increasing quantities and qualities of service.

Friends once told me of an experience they had in a large department store. They learned in talking with a salesperson that the item they were looking for was not available. The salesperson called the company's competitor and inquired about the item. The other business had it on hand. My friends found their item at the other store, but they will return to the first store for future purchases because they found a remarkable attitude of service.

The vision of service must never be forgotten, or we risk severing our partnership with God. If the vision is forgotten, mistakes and poor decisions will increase, rather than new services. The desire for profits and dividends rather than service causes a company to toil and spin.

Toxic dumping and cover-ups of unsafe mechanical systems and practices are evidence of a crumbling circle without a center. In these companies, the entrepreneurial spirit and innovation are dying. The future is struggle and then collapse. Rather than respond quickly to the needs of society, these businesses move like lumbering giants, often harming those in their paths. Rather than assume responsibility for wrongdoing or mistakes, these companies choose to try to hide mistakes and serve themselves. Money is of greater value than integrity and public safety. Such enterprises fail. Nothing can endure that is not in partnership with God, and a partnership with God cannot fail.

Value #3

"We have the mind of Christ" (1 Cor. 2:16). We have within us the wisdom of the ages and therefore the ability to see clearly and act wisely. The challenge is releasing this "imprisoned splendor." In a business, it is the work of leadership to create an atmosphere that allows the wisdom to be expressed. The twenty-first-century business will be a place of creativity.

Accessing the wisdom within each associate will take place on many levels. Most workers have a sense of how to most effectively accomplish their tasks. Why not ask them? In many companies, this is usually done for a time, and then it is business as usual. The key is to foster a consciousness of creativity, so there must be a continuous search for new ways of doing things and new ways of serving.

Another approach to releasing the "imprisoned splendor" is to allow people the time to think. Businesses are often so driven to get the work done that they fail to realize the ideas which keep a company on the leading edge require "think time." A company may have a research and development department, but the effectiveness of an enterprise can often be increased in many other areas of the operation. Why not give the associates the time to ponder such things? For too long, business has relegated creativity to a select few. This leaves untapped a reservoir of practical ideas and denies the fundamental value that we all have the Mind of the Christ.

I know of a company that provides a room and time for its associates to get away from the job during the day. It is not just a place to think; it is a place to release stress and find peace. When leadership knows that each person is a wellspring of wisdom, not only will there be think time, but anything that is a barrier to the release of the inner wisdom will be addressed.

Stress is a great barrier to creativity. Human beings encounter stress on a daily basis. Stress is not the problem. Problems mount and stress builds when we feel alone and that no one cares about us. Creativity dies when we believe ourselves unable to deal with the stress and challenges of daily living.

I can remember a place where I used to work. Individuals who tried to share their challenges and asked for help were told, "That sounds like a personal problem." The statement indicated that personal problems and one's profession were not to meet. My observation has been that they meet every day.

Society has ordained certain places for people to get help and specific people like clergy, social workers, and psychologists to do the helping. The business community's approach has been that it is not concerned with a worker's personal life as long as it does not interfere with the job. If it does interfere, the worker is to get help, get fixed, and then do the job he or she was hired to do.

Business in the twenty-first century will not separate person and profession. It will care about the associate as well as the job. Already this is happening. Wellness and fitness programs, daycare for children, and liberal vacation schedules are being made available to associates. In the future there will be more opportunities for individuals to grow and rise above their human problems. Esteem and self-worth will grow, and barriers to creativity will diminish.

The end result of such practices is that the people who serve in the company feel valued. No one is more important than anyone else. The president may seem more important than others because he or she makes decisions that impact the direction and effectiveness of the business, but so does everyone else. What is the fate of a company that does not fill its orders on time? What will happen to a business if the receptionist is rude to clients?

The most effective businesses of our new century will be people-oriented—not just the people served—but the associates who do the bulk of the work. Pay, benefits, revenue sharing, and training are important, but these will not satisfy a spiritual being. People of vision want more. They want to be able to make a contribution to the direction of the business and the services offered to the world. We are at our best when we are asked to release the wisdom that is within us.

This means inviting people from every level in the organization to participate in brainstorming and creative thinking. This values the people and declares that each associate has the Mind of the Christ. However, not all people allow the wisdom that is within them to be expressed. Poor self-image and unhealed past experiences with authority figures often do not permit the person to express his or her potential. Every opportunity should be afforded associates, so they might discover and then express who they are, although this does not mean that incompetence or insubordination is acceptable. While the twenty-first-century enterprise is responsible to live out its ideals, the twenty-first-century associate is also responsible for many things.

Responsibilities of a 21st-Century Associate

Each associate is responsible for knowing the vision and purpose of the organization. The spiritual entrepreneur knows the value of vision because it is the originating force of the business. Initially, through an orientation program, new associates are told about the vision and the company's ideals. Through continued communication, the vision is kept before the associates.

Each associate is responsible for working from an attitude of service. It is said that we have moved from the industrial age into an information age which calls for an ever-increasing number of service industries. This is not true. Service has always been the heart of business regardless of the age. Even when the city market was the primary place to conduct business, service was a valued commodity. Each associate is responsible for working from an attitude of service because the vision of any successful business is to serve others and help them fulfill their needs.

Each associate is responsible for allowing the "imprisoned splendor" to be expressed. The life worth living is a creative life. Because we are made in God's image, nothing needs to be added to us; however, there is much to be released from within. The leadership of a business has the responsibility of creating an atmosphere where people can express their "imprisoned splendor," and it is the responsibility of the associate to share this wisdom for the common good.

Each associate is responsible for allowing the healing of his or her unresolved issues. We do not always express our true nature. Often when we believe ourselves less than we want to be, we blame others. In our professional lives, we may blame the company or our supervisor. For instance, an unresolved hurt with a parent often appears as a conflict with an authority figure at work—our supervisor. As children, we try to get the approval of our parents. In some cases, through no fault of the child, the parent does not express approval. This little one may grow into an adult who believes that the job description says to get the boss' approval. This is not true. We have a series of tasks to perform. This is our work, not approval seeking. Looking for approval is only one of the potential blocks to a successful career and life. However, regardless of the blockage, it is the responsibility of the associate to alleviate that which imprisons the wisdom within.

It is possible that we may be free of past hurts, but find ourselves in a company which does not value the creativity of its associates. If this happens, we are not to blame the company or any individual. As spiritual beings, we are not victims. If we are not allowed to express creatively, we have the option to leave the organization and be who we are.

Each associate is responsible for working from an attitude of trust. Even in a company that diligently communicates with its associates, it is not possible for everyone to know the reason why all things are done the way they are. Trust is needed, for decisions and policies will not always make sense to everyone. The important thing is for leadership to make a diligent effort to live the vision and ideals that are the company's foundation.

It is also vital that the leadership and associates be allowed to be human. No company member appreciates being held so accountable for behavior that he or she cannot be human. All of us make mistakes and poor decisions. When we make mistakes, this does not mean we cannot be trusted anymore. It means we are human and need the support of others more than ever. It is the responsibility of leadership and associates to trust one another and to work from an attitude of trust.

Each associate is responsible to be a growing, ever-unfolding individual. In the twenty-first-century business, each person is called to do more than punch the clock and do the job. The associate will be nurtured and supported as never before. This is not just a matter of better pay and benefits. The leadership and associates are expected to be true to their nature. This is a call to grow.

This does not mean that we must be religious or adhere to a creed of particular beliefs. The call is for us to express our potential. When we retire, we must be more than we were the first day we came to work. In the past, whether this happened or not was our responsibility. This will not change, but the associate of the twenty-first century will have the support of the company.

Many of us live for our job. It becomes our life and identity—who we are. In the twentieth century, a company would want such associates, for they are hardworking and loyal, but in the twenty-first century, this will not be true. The best associates will work hard and be loyal to the company, but their identity will not be in what they do.

Our identity and worth cannot be in earthly things, for they change. If our identity is in our job, what happens when we lose our job or retire? What are we then? As we grow, we will eventually find our identity in Spirit, and we and the company will be better because of this.

Each associate is responsible for looking to God as the source rather than the company. The company of the twenty-first century will serve its associates in ever-increasing ways. Innovation, which is the heart of any successful enterprise, will not be applied solely to servicing the community. Associates are an important group of people to be served. However, it is paramount that leadership and associates not look to the business as the source or as supply. The company or its customers may seem to be the source, and the monthly or bimonthly paycheck may appear to be supply, but this is not true. *God is the source, and a consciousness of God is the supply.* Each associate is responsible to know this with deep conviction.

A Debt-Free 21st Century

Indebtedness is considered by many to be our primary block to prosperous living; however, debt is a fact of life in today's society. Many of us spend nearly our whole lives in debt to some institution. It is clear that financial ruin can come to any company or individual whose debts are not paid. The good news is that the debt we or a company may owe in the twenty-first century is not the important issue.

From a spiritual perspective, debt is not owing money to an individual or financial institution. True debt occurs when we think we cannot pay the debt or begrudge the fact that we must pay. True debt is a thought of lack, and it must be paid.

Understanding this principle, Charles Fillmore shares an interesting viewpoint on indebtedness in his book *Prosperity.* Fillmore states that it is possible for the creditor, the one who is owed money, to go in debt to the debtor.

This occurs when accounts are receivable, but payment is not forthcoming. The creditor then begins to think lack—his focus is on what he does not have. If the one owed money continues to think in this way, he, too, goes into debt, for indebtedness is not just owing money to another; it is allowing one's consciousness to be filled with lack.

This debt must be paid. The trend of negative

thinking and focus upon what is not received must cease. Fillmore points out that the creditor should bless the debtor and know the Truth about this person. Thinking ill thoughts about the individual or company is not helpful. Many a creditor has found that after he or she ceased focusing upon what was owed, bills were paid.

This is a healthy approach for the leadership of any business. A long time ago, I read a story about a man who was owed money. He sent out notices requesting payment, but nothing happened. This greatly disturbed him. Finally, a solution came to mind. He wrote the debtor and told him of his upset, blessed him, and forgave the bill.

From a pure business standpoint, this solution made no sense. From a spiritual perspective, it was an ideal solution. The creditor realized that his consciousness of lack and resentment had become a barrier to his prosperity. He may have lost the funds due him, but he would have lost much more if he had continued in his state of indebtedness. By revealing his feelings to the man who owed the money, but also by blessing him and forgiving the debt, the creditor freed himself. The interesting conclusion to the story is that after learning of the forgiven debt, the debtor paid the bill.

We can allow our consciousness to be filled with thoughts of lack when we begrudge paying our bills. Lack dominates our life when we live beyond our means and struggle in making ends meet. We think lack because we do not have what another owes us. Successful endeavors have sown the seeds of failure by thinking in this way. Lack is insidious regardless of how it begins. This debt must be paid.

Responsibilities of the Immensely Wealthy

A successful business blesses many people: customers, vendors, associates, leadership, and community. Often the leadership earns millions of dollars each year, more money than can realistically be spent on oneself. With the increase in salary, there can be an enlarged appetite for worldly things. Houses can be bought, expensive cars purchased, diamonds and precious works of art obtained, but the spiritual entrepreneur of the twenty-first century will use wealth in a different way.

The immensely wealthy are not to be centers of consumption, but centers that redistribute wealth for the common good. Just as it was for the business, this begins with vision.

Sir John Marks Templeton, as mentioned in Chapter Four, is an immensely wealthy man who has made a fortune in investments. His success and farsightedness are admired by many, but it is his vision and ideals, reflected in the Templeton Foundation Prize for Progress in Religion, that set him apart from other individuals who are immensely wealthy.

Ewing M. Kauffman of Kansas City, Missouri, who died in 1993, is another forerunner for the twenty-first-century spiritual entrepreneur whose vision and ideals serve to bless many.

The Kauffman Foundation was founded to fund various programs to help children and entrepreneurs. One of the programs, "Project Choice," pays for the college or vocational education of graduated high school seniors from the inner city who have maintained their grades and remained drug-free during their high school careers. "Project Early" helps families and agencies provide prenatal and early intervention for the benefit of children. "Project Essential" attempts to help children earn and maintain self-esteem and overcome external, social barriers.

Both Templeton and Kauffman have exhibited rich spirits. They have worked hard and have been people of vision and consequently have been a blessing and example to humanity. This is possible for all of us, but it is essential for those who are immensely wealthy in an earthly sense. In this age, money has a higher purpose than meeting tangible needs. Because of the way our society is structured, people of vision can help turn money into changed lives. For Templeton and Kauffman, money has had a heavenly purpose—to help humanity discover its potential.

Gathered in His Name

The twenty-first-century business will be a partnership with God. The spiritual entrepreneur and associates will be unified by vision and high ideals. They will gather in His name, and something incredible will be released from their midst. "For where two or three are gathered in my name, there am I in the midst of them" (Mt. 18:20). Service and creativity will be the watchwords of this partnership dedicated to the common good.

Each person, whether the chief executive officer or the entry-level associate, will be a window through which the values of the company can be seen. The ideals will be evident in the boardroom and in the stockroom. The vision will come through the president presenting an address at a business symposium and the receptionist greeting visitors.

Key Ideas

1. Money and career are not our reason for being.
2. People with the highest ideals make the greatest contribution to humanity.
3. Our career is an outpicturing of our heartfelt beliefs and values.
4. Vision and service are one in a successful enterprise.

5. The twenty-first-century business will be a place of creativity.
6. Responsibilities of the Twenty-First-Century Associate:
    - to know the vision and purpose of the organization
    - to work from an attitude of service
    - to allow the "imprisoned splendor" to be expressed
    - to allow the healing of his or her unresolved issues
    - to work from an attitude of trust
    - to be a growing, ever-unfolding individual
    - to look to God as the source, not to the company
7. Debt is a thought of lack.
8. A successful business blesses its customers, vendors, associates, leadership, and community.

Affirmation

God is my partner.

Summary

My work and vision are service.

SECTION THREE

The Coming Vision

The spiritual principles outlined in Section One of this book can transform an individual's life, but we are not one person; we are many. It is not enough that one of us prospers. All of us must know security and well-being. Imagine what would happen if the people of a community, the citizens of every nation, and eventually all the inhabitants of our planet knew that God was their source and that a consciousness of God was their supply.

The following three chapters speculate on the transformation of our world; they are different in format than the preceding chapters. May they stimulate our thinking and cause compassion to break forth from our hearts. In this way, a new vision will sweep across the Earth.

In it, lack will perish from every community, poverty from all nations, and famines from the lands. Then we will know the balance of earthly living and a spiritual life. The vision will dawn person by person. A child who would have died of malnutrition will live, and this child will find the cure for our deadliest disease. Another person who would have perished will give birth to a musician who will compose music that makes our hearts sing. On and on it goes. One life transformed, and it transforms us all.

CHAPTER
10

Poverty, Plenty, and Paradise

The "I" Has Seen the "We"

The world has many needs, but its greatest need is to discover and to consciously put into practice the prosperity principles that have fed, clothed, and brought security and inner peace to the human family during its ascending spiral of evolution and progress. Not only will these laws of life put bread on the table of every human being, they will also provide security and well-being that transcend what we possess. And out of the God-inspired security will come creativity and the expression of our divine potential that blesses the Earth.

There is great wealth in the world. There are immensely wealthy nations and rich individuals whose net worth exceeds that of countries, but there is also inexcusable poverty. The *Human Development Report 1998* reveals that "of the 4.4 billion people in developing countries, nearly three-fifths lack access to sanitation, a third have no access to clean water, a quarter do not have adequate housing and a fifth have no access to modern health services of any kind . . . with 3.6 billion suffering from iron deficiency, 2 billion of whom are anemic."[1] The report continues: "About 17 million people in developing countries die each year from such curable infectious and parasitic diseases as diarrhea, measles, malaria, and tuberculosis."[2] Even the United States, "with the highest average income . . . , has the highest population share experiencing human poverty" in the industrialized world.[3]

Poverty is the problem of those in need, but it is also the problem of those who have much. We are in this together, and although another country may not be our nation's primary trading partner or produce goods that we feel we need, their need is still the problem of any nation of caring people. A global economy is emerging. No great wall can isolate one culture from another. No nation can be an island unto itself and produce a false economy that prospers its people. Even the economies of the world are beginning to reflect the spiritual Truth that we are one.

Many of us have seen pictures of the Earth as

the astronauts have seen it—a luminous blue and white pearl hanging in the heavens without borders or division. The "I" has seen the "we," and consequently, we can never be the same. The global economy is also forcing us to see ourselves as one. Even our desires are helping to weave us together. It was this way in the time before history when tribes traded goods with one another. Now the tribes are nations. Eventually, the nations will become one world, for we are one people with one Creator.

Diversity's Role in Oneness

We need not only the goods that others create; we need one another. We may want a particular product, but there is nothing to buy unless a skilled person or persons create it. However, we must look at one another as more than the producer or the consumer of goods.

In the future the experience of oneness will be a central breakthrough enabling us to truly prosper and to find security. A world economy and common needs help to bring us together, but the power of oneness is brought to bear when we honor and celebrate our diversity. As long as we persist in declaring *our* culture, religion, or way of doing things right and the culture, religion, or approach to life of another person wrong, we will not prosper or find security. Our need to be right and to make another wrong is the seed of war. A world that fails to celebrate the differences of its inhabitants is a world in conflict, and conflict makes security and prosperity impossible.

Conflict destroys the infrastructure of a country and its human resources. "Over the past decade armed conflict has killed 2 million children, disabled 4–5 million, and left 12 million homeless, more than 1 million orphaned or separated from their parents and some 10 million psychologically traumatized."[4] We are all richer when we are willing to discover why a culture has developed the way it has developed. When we know why people value certain things, we are richer for it. In fact, our values may shift, and we may find a better way of doing things. And, of course, we may learn ways that would not work for us.

There is no awareness of oneness without the celebration of diversity. Just as an individual cannot prosper and find true security when he or she is unable to work in harmony with coworkers, so, too, are nations unable to truly prosper when they are in conflict with each other.

It seems that part of our problem is that we tend to stereotype other countries and cultures. For instance, Americans often think of Muslims as religious fanatics and Iraqis as fools for following Sadam Hussein, but when we get to know individuals from other lands, we begin to see a greater depth than what the news media portrays. We begin to understand why people act and react the way they do.

We are fortunate in the United States because we have so many cultures and viewpoints represented throughout the American landscape. It is part of what makes the nation great. By taking the time to study and become aware of people of different ethnic and national origins, we explore diversity and take one more step toward an experience of oneness.

Those who are able to travel to other countries have opportunities to see differences as unique expressions of God's divine plan. Cultural exchanges likewise seed the planet with a consciousness that is willing to embrace diversity. I suspect that although the state departments of the various countries of the world receive credit whenever nations are joined in a unity of purpose, it is the ordinary people of the nations who are the statespersons who have done the quiet work of opening themselves to new possibilities.

An Example of Statespeople at Work

In 1899 Argentina and Chile were moving steadily toward armed conflict. During Easter of the next year most Chileans and Argentineans thought war was a certainty. On Easter day, Monsignor Benavente preached a sermon in Buenos Aires. He cried out for peace. A bishop in Chile heard of the sermon and opened the heart of his people with a similar appeal for harmony. Slowly a momentum began to build. The consciousness of the people of the two countries that had always lived in peace forced the two governments to submit their border dispute to King Edward VII of Great Britain for arbitration.

The dispute was resolved, and another step was taken that was an example to the world. The weapons poised on the border were melted down and cast into a large bronze statue of Jesus. The image was carried on gun carriages to the 13,000-foot level of the mountainous border between the two countries. Soldiers and sailors took the statue the final distance and erected it on March 13, 1904. These words were inscribed as an example of the work that oneness can do: "These mountains themselves shall fall and crumble to dust before the people of Chile and the Argentine Republic forget their solemn covenant sworn at the feet of Christ." In addition, the following scripture was included because it defined the moment of their unity, "He is our peace, who hath made both one" (Eph. 2:14 KJV).

We are one in Spirit, and the forces of the universe are gently compelling us to know and experience our oneness. Our existence ultimately will be determined because of our willingness to find the beauty in our seeming differences and our oneness in our varied cultures and religions, and this discovery will prosper the world and all its people.

One in Body and Soul

Years ago I was reading the April 17, 1996, *USA Today* newspaper. In the health section, I came across a headline that intrigued me: "Viruses mutate among underfed." The article began, "Malnourished people . . . may provide a breeding ground for dangerous mutant viruses that then can be passed along and cause illness in otherwise healthy people, scientists report today." The article continued by detailing the research of virologist Dr. Melinda Beck of the University of North Carolina. The implications of her studies conducted in the laboratory mice concerned other scientists.

For years scientists have known that undernourished people are more susceptible to disease than those individuals who eat a nutritious, balanced diet. Now it seems that viruses that are ordinarily not a threat to healthy individuals can mutate in a malnourished body to form a strain of the disease that can infect otherwise healthy individuals. This may explain why new illnesses seem to originate in third world countries.

Dr. Orville A. Levander, a nutritionist with the U.S. Department of Agriculture, says, "We are our brother's keeper because we're not protected from what might be happening to malnourished people in Africa."

There is a need for the industrialized world to reach out to those in need. We are in this together. We cannot turn our backs on what is happening in Africa or any other country. We are united in body and soul.

It is a basic human right to have enough to eat, safe water to drink, sanitary conditions in which to live, and access to health care and education. The *Human Development Report of 1998* describes the world in 2050 as being populated by 9.5 billion people, 8 billion of which will be living in poor countries.[5] This is our trend—most of the world living in poverty, but it does not have to be. The report continues that Americans spend more on cosmetics, $8 billion annually, and the Europeans more on ice cream, $11 billion annually, than is estimated it would cost to provide basic education, $6 billion, and sanitation, $9 billion, for all the inhabitants of the world. Worldwide basic health and nutrition would cost $13 billion. This contrasts sharply with the $17 billion spent on pet foods in the United States and Europe. And, of course, there is the $780 billion spent around the world on military spending because we do not yet celebrate our diversity or know our oneness.[6]

We Have the Means; Do We Have the Will?

We have the means to make a profound impact on human conditions. The question is, Do we have the strength and the will to establish the necessary new priorities? It is understandable, but interesting, that we will rush to the aid of countries whose economies directly affect our own, but we do not assist countries whose economies have little effect upon our consumer society. However, when the Truth of oneness dawns in us, and we return to the image of the Earth that hangs in the heaven, one without borders or divisions, we will realize that the plight of others is our plight as well.

Who can be content when the need for sharing is so apparent? In Islam, it is written: "Riches are not from an abundance of worldly good, but from a contented mind." Taoism declares: "He who knows he has enough is rich." This is what we need—a new understanding of riches and wealth. And we need to heed the message we learned as children— share what you have with one another. Every reluctant child ultimately discovers the joys of giving and of playing in harmony with others. Every reluctant adult will also discover the joy of giving and the wonders of growth that come because the adult has cared for others.

Eden Will Come Again

Earth can be a paradise. Many people wait for divine intervention. They anticipate a savior or deliverer who will bring peace and plenty to the world. I suspect that when we are still and listen to the divine wisdom that resides in us, it is saying: "Peace is not mine to bring to you. Peace is present now. It is yours when you honor your differences and discover your oneness. And as you find the beauty in your diversity and share with one another, Eden will come again. Not only will you help one another live; you will help one another give expression to all that I am. This is My plan. Make it your own and poverty will end, not solely because you have food to eat and water to drink, but because you are rich in your love for one another."

Notes

1. *Human Development Report 1998,* United Nations Development Programme, Oxford University Press, New York, Oxford, 1998, p. 50.
2. *Ibid.,* p. 50.
3. *Ibid.,* p. 2.
4. *Ibid.,* p. 35.
5. *Ibid.,* p. 66.
6. *Ibid.,* p. 37.

CHAPTER
11

The Emerging
Homo Simplicitus

"In God We Trust"

Spiritual principles can be applied to all areas of life. For instance, the ideas shared in this book will work in an individual's life, in a business, and in a ministry. I believe that their practicality can also extend to a nation's financial well-being and to the emerging global economy which binds all the countries of the world together.

America is currently considered to be the most prosperous country in the world. From the viewpoint of many economic indicators, this is true. We have the largest budget on Earth, over $1.7 trillion.[1] The per capita personal income of approximately

$25,000 is the highest in the world.[2] Our output of goods and services is unparalleled in human history.

Why is America so prosperous? What factors contribute to the nation's ongoing success? Fundamentally, the United States has a system of government that encourages its people to pursue their dreams and to develop and use their talents. Although the nation does not publicly affirm God to be its source or a consciousness of God to be its supply, there is a declared faith that is evident in the imprint on the country's coin and currency: "In God we trust." This was the consciousness of America's founders, and today it remains a part of the religious and spiritual life of the nation. Another contributing factor is that since America's early beginnings, most of the nation's leaders have been prosperous people. They bring a consciousness of plenty to the halls of Congress and into the White House.

America appears to be a giving nation. The president's fiscal year 1997 budget included $12.3 billion for foreign aid.[3] This is a sizable sum of money, but it is less than 1 percent of the overall budget. And in many cases, this giving is not an expression of the spiritual nature of the country's people; it is an instrument of foreign policy. Strings are attached because something is sought in return. This kind of giving does not put God first; it puts the nation's interests first. Giving that anticipates a return is prevalent because there is a pervading belief in the nation's consciousness that money has power. This is thought to be a strength, but actually it is one of America's weaknesses. Money is not power, nor is it supply.

The Strength of Any Nation

The strength of any nation is its people. America's founding fathers devised a system of government that, in theory, calls forth the potential of its people. This ideal has not yet been realized, but it is consistent with the divine plan that calls forth the expression of God from within each individual. In Truth, the collective consciousness of the people prospers the nation. Triumphs and dangers flow from this maxim. For instance, one of the great enemies of divine expression is fear. The economic impact of fear is easily seen when the stock market experiences a massive loss of its value. October 24, 1929, marked the beginning of the stock market's first crash as millions of people withdrew their money in fear of losing it all. Many did. Since that first Black Thursday, there have been a series of "black days" in which prices plummeted. October 27, 1997, was declared a Black Monday as the Dow Jones Industrial average fell 550 points or just over 7 percent of its value.[4] Often economic indicators remain excellent; nevertheless there is panic selling, and the value of stocks decreases by millions of dollars in a single day. The movement of the stock market tracks to some degree the confidence of the people and their ability to stand firm in the face of appearances.

Underlying the fear is the concern that we will lose what we have acquired. This brings us to a revelation that can ultimately place the nation upon a path which leads to true security and well-being. One of the greatest principles of prosperity is that we demonstrate prosperity by giving rather than getting. The problem in America is that we have become a consumer society. Getting is the consciousness of the nation. Acquisition and holding on to what we have acquired is the national pastime. Eric Fromm's *Homo consumens*, the total consumer, rules the day and the night.

More is better and *shop 'til ya drop* are more than clichés when we discover that the average American consumes 18 tons of natural resources each year.[5] In fact, we consume twice as much today as we did forty years ago, but there is no reported increase in happiness.[6] The number of people reporting to be happy has declined during this period.

Acquisition and our identity have merged. Success is measured by what we have rather than what we have given, by our purchases rather than what we produce. Economic councils and company executives certainly do not view us as spiritual beings; sometimes they do not even see us as a people. We are called consumers, and regrettably, their description is accurate. In addition, collectively, we are not people, we are the "market." Goods are not offered to us, they are marketed to us. Children between the ages of 4 and 12 are a $9 billion market.[7] Teenagers are a $93 billion market.[8] This is the kind of economy and society we have created.

A consumer society is bombarded by advertising because the economy is driven by consumption. Without increased buying, it falters. Every day, 18 billion display ads appear in magazines and newspapers across the country.[9] In fact, in most cases the print media is sustained by the advertising revenue rather than subscriptions. Fourteen billion catalogs are mailed to potential consumers every year.[10] (I think I personally receive 7 billion!) In 1994 the collective advertising expenditure in the nation was $148 billion.[11] This is more than the 1990 reported Gross Domestic Product of the top twenty economies in the world. We have more shopping centers than high schools. The sheer volume of the advertising is immense, but from a spiritual perspective, its message is what is most disturbing. Promises of loving relationships, fame, self-esteem, and prosperity are made if we will buy the product. If we consume, we will be happy and fulfilled.

And so we consume, but we are not happy. The signs are all around us. We do not even feel secure. This is one of the reasons we must have more and more. A way of life has been created that is fundamentally flawed. I believe we sense that there is a problem, but we are addicted to acquisition. We have not found a better way.

As I write, I realize that I must heed what I have written, for I, too, am caught in the web of acquisition and consumption. Flowing from within me are words that anyone in the nation could have written because we know that something is amiss. When fulfillment and even love are tied to what we acquire, there is a problem. The good news is that there is an answer. Eventually Homo consumens will falter, and *Homo simplicitus* will emerge.

Homo Simplicitus

Every nation has either its elected or self-appointed leaders, but the true leadership of any country is its people. History records times of revolution and the overthrow of kings, dictators, and governments, but even when the people do not rise up, they still determine the direction that becomes the future and eventually the history of the country.

If we are to experience true security and well-being, we must lead the way. I believe the evidence of change is with us now. Please note that acquisition is not denied its place in daily life, but it is assigned its *proper* place. It is important that acquisition not be denied because whenever there is denial of something basic to human nature, there is usually an unwholesome expression. Therefore, in the future we will not deny ourselves the joys of human expression, but we will not allow these pleasures to dominate our inner or outer lives. Let us pose again Jesus' question: "For what will it profit a man, if he gains the whole world and forfeits his life?" (Mt. 16:26)

Where there is a truly prosperous nation and truly prosperous people, there is simplicity. Simplicity appears to be living with less, but this does not mean depriving ourselves of some of the nice things of life; it is living in a way that allows us to be true to our spiritual nature. Simplicity is living out of one's highest values.

People are beginning to do this. They are giving up career opportunities in order to spend more time with their families or turning avocations into vocations. They are going back to school to train to do what they have always wanted to do rather than what they felt compelled to do by their parents, or so they could make a six-figure salary. They are rising above the harried lifestyle of the consumer. They don't work so they can make purchases or so they can retire, relax, and play. Their work supports the causes they value. Moments are not filled solely with activity; they are filled with meaning.

No one just decides to live a simpler life. The real issue is determining what is important. What do we value? The question is not what are we willing to die for, but what are we willing to live for? A few core values are discovered, then lived. There is simplicity because our values clarify our reason for being, what is important to us, and therefore what we do.

We need a national leader who lives a simple life and who simply lives. The happiness radiating from this person would enliven us and serve as an example of the way life could be lived. In recent history, Ghandi stood as a supreme example of a simple life that grows from a few basic core values. He valued freedom. He valued work as evidenced by his daily spinning of cloth. He valued spirituality. He valued standing firm against injustice armed only with nonresistance. These values stoked the fire of his passion for India and its people. What he held dear provided him with the inner resources that enabled him to touch the hearts of people around the world and to cause the British empire to release India to its own destiny.

Living in Balance, Balancing the Budget

People who live simply do not live beyond their means. They may use credit as a tool, but not as a means to keep up with the Joneses or as a way to prop up their self-image or to attempt to fill their emptiness. Their values do not demand that they buy a larger house or car. Their purchases rise out of their values. Homo simplicitus' security and well-being rest not in having more, but in wisely using what they have.

It is interesting that people often acquire what they feel they must have only to suffer under the weight of their own thoughts about the debts they have accumulated. They have purchased a new thing, but they are thinking lack. The limiting thoughts and the feelings they create make it impossible to enjoy the purchased item.

Many years ago my family lived in a beautiful house. A staircase wound around a large tree that was illumined by a skylight from above. The house was grand and beautiful, but it was a burden. We made our payments, but felt limited. Our thoughts of lack came to fruition when we sold the house and lost $20,000. It was a graphic reminder of living out of balance.

The United States lives beyond its means. It is easy to point to the country's national debt, but the personal public debt as of September 17, 1998, was $5.5 trillion.[12] Obviously, our lawmakers take their lead from us. The national debt is a manifestation of Homo consumens and the consumer society in which we live.

A headline in a midwestern newspaper read, "Unabashed Americans are spending more." The subheading read, "Economists express concern as weakness abroad seems certain to force cutbacks in U.S." Economic downturns cause us to cut back for a time, but the consumer society lives to shop. However, I believe a new species of human is being born. Compassion rather than consumption is the work of this being. While Homo consumens defines itself by its net worth, the new species, Homo simplicitus, defines itself by its search for its own soul.

Notes

1. "Reinventing America II: Budget of the United States, FY 1997," [http://www.crossover.com/reus/cmt.html], 1 October 1998.

2. "Texas Department of Human Services," [http://bms.dhs.state.tx.us/reports/Glance/96Fall/PCPI.html], 1 October 1998.

3. "Reinventing America II: Budget of the United States, FY 1997."

4. Mark Zandi, "Global Stock Market Contagion," [http://www.dismal.com/thoughts/crash2.stm], 28 October 1997.

5. Jonathan Harris, "Consumption and the Environment," in *The Consumer Society.* Series ed. Neva R. Goodwin (Island Press, 1997), p. 269.

6. Alan Durning, "Asking How Much Is Enough," in *The Consumer Society.* Series ed. Neva R. Goodwin (Island Press, 1997), p. 11.

7. David Kiron and Seymour Bellin, "Family, Gender, and Socialization," in *The Consumer Society.* Series ed. Neva R. Goodwin (Island Press, 1997), p. 84.

8. *Ibid.*

9. David Kiron, "Perpetuating Consumer Culture: Media, Advertising, and Wants Creation," in *The Consumer Society.* Series ed. Neva R. Goodwin (Island Press, 1997), p. 229.

10. *Ibid.,* p. 230.

11. *Ibid.*

12. "The Public Debt to the Penny," [http://www.publicdebt.treas.gov/opd/opdpenny.htm], 22 December 1998.

CHAPTER
12

The Beginning of the End of Poverty

There is poverty in the world and great need in every nation. This human suffering seems far away as it is beamed into our houses through satellite technology. However, a short drive from our homes, there are people in need, those who have little to eat, whose only clothing is what they wear, and who have no home in which to raise their children. In every community, there are those who have much and those who have little. In fact, the *Human Development Report of 1998* reveals, as previously noted, that there is more poverty in the United States than in any other industrialized nation in the world. Our per capita income is the highest in the world, and yet in the communities of the American fiscal giant, there is poverty that stretches from generation to generation.

It is easy to say that those in need must become aware that God is their source and that it is their consciousness which must be transformed, but what of the consciousness of those whose bellies are full, yet do nothing to banish poverty from their community? Of all the "projects" that humankind could jointly undertake, the eradication of poverty from the face of the Earth is the most achievable goal and the most far-reaching in its impact upon the human family. Poverty is affecting people's lives every day. Human potential is unrealized, and therefore we all suffer. Perhaps it is the boy or girl living in poverty in Bangladesh, in Belfast, or in our community who has the capacity to discover the cure for the most current incurable disease or a safe, inexhaustible energy source.

Poverty and its adjoining problems of malnutrition and disease have plagued humankind for thousands of years. War has been declared upon poverty, but it remains undefeated. Must it always be with us? Now, perhaps more than at any other time in history, we have the ability to banish poverty from the planet. The question is, Will we do it?

Prosperity Begins With the Individual

Prosperity begins with us. Spiritual principles govern our lives, and when they are discovered and put into practice in daily life, we experience security and a state of well-being that transcend conditions. This is the way it has always been. First, there is an awareness of the underlying spiritual principles that govern an aspect of our lives. Then the principles are tested and proven in the same way that the premises of science are verified through careful experimentation. A scientific researcher is usually detached and not personally impacted by the result of the experiment. In the testing of spiritual principles, this is not the case. Each person becomes the discoverer and the researcher conducting the experiment. The individual's life is directly impacted by the result of trying to put into practice a spiritual principle. The good news is that once the experiment is conducted and proven, the individual knows its validity from personal experience. This individual now speaks with authority. He or she knows what is true and the impact that the spiritual principle can have upon daily life. The individual is respected not for making money but for being in concert with the spiritual laws that govern the universe and the lives of all people. This individual is highly qualified to work within the community and make a difference.

One of the first experiences of community can be in the family. A good place to start is giving. When a family tithes, it is an opportunity for the whole family, including the children, to determine where the tithe will be given. These monthly "tithe meetings" can be the most meaningful time that a family can share. A consciousness of giving is created, and it becomes a seed for the future security of the children as well as the beginning of a deeper understanding of the law of giving and receiving. In addition, a family can decide to assist in a community project that brings the family members face-to-face with those in need.

When a person decides to assist in helping those who are in need, there is the possibility of two of the most profound breakthroughs that a human being can experience—an insight into human suffering and a great surge of joy. There is no greater feeling of exuberance than helping someone while asking for nothing in return. Even though the feeling of exhilaration is grand, there is more. Growth in consciousness results, and the person who renders the help is transformed and expanded. It is for this reason that the servants of humankind have come to see that the needs of others are actually gifts. They are precious, and when properly received not only are needs met, souls expand. The person in need discovers that he or she is worthy and precious to others and to God. The servant sees needs differently; they are often the only gift that some people can give. To fail to accept their gift is a great travesty. Regrettably, the gift of need is being rejected in every community on Earth.

Their Gift Is Their Need

Have you ever been at the bedside of a dying person whose life has been lived in service of others? Currently this person can do little for himself or herself even though he or she used to do much for others—even a drink of water requires assistance, or the lips must be moistened with cream or lip balm. Usually, the person dislikes this helpless state, but for the family or friends who are assisting, it can be a precious time. They are needed, and it is wonderful to serve those who have served for so many years. In many instances, eventually the person whose last days draw near comes to understand that even helplessness is one more way of giving and serving.

Anyone can break through into this new understanding of need. In today's society, many individuals are not part of a traditional family; however, each of us is part of a large family called the community in which we live. Service clubs abound, and organizations are always in search of competent volunteers who are willing to go the extra mile. Friends can join together and decide to accept the gift of need that is extended by many of the individuals in the community.

This is the way transformation begins. First, someone discovers, puts to the test, and finally lives the spiritual principles that govern our lives. Second, this person sees needs for what they are—gifts. A new understanding of the nature of need and the awareness of the underlying spirituality of our humanity naturally lead to the next step—action.

Christmas is a traditional time when we think of "those less fortunate than ourselves." In churches that I served, we always initiated a "Christmas project" during the holidays but we never ceased giving when the "season" ended. We continued the project indefinitely, and the next year we added another project. We began by collecting food for the local agencies. Another year we began to serve in the local soup kitchen that fed the children who lived on the streets. We assisted adults in learning to read. We became a resource for the local blood bank. Every year a new project began and more and more people were given the opportunity to serve the needs of individuals and the community.

Opportunities to Give

America is a giving nation. We have many social agencies whose purpose is to help those in need. Many of their methods have proved effective throughout the years. However, perhaps it is time to consider alternatives that engage the community and provide opportunities for more people to begin to see a need as a gift.

The following is a list of possible projects that would help to eliminate poverty in a local community. I trust that some of these ideas are currently being enacted in villages, towns, and cities around the world.

1. Every day, in every city, restaurants throw away unserved food, but there are also networks of people who gather the food and distribute it to people in need. How difficult would it be for a restaurant owner to provide one more casserole for the volunteer to take where it would help to feed hungry people?

2. Periodic "Circulation Days" could be conducted in communities. A circulation project begins when people identify those items in their household that they are not using. (These items have been "out of circulation" for at least a year.) The items are brought to a central location, and the community is invited to come and take what they need. It is important that volunteers be carefully trained to allow for those individuals who will take advantage of the situation such as flea market dealers. These professionals are to be supported as well. There are two main ingredients to a circulation day: giving and receiving. The community is invited to come and take what it needs. However, the individuals should also be given the opportunity to return to their

homes and return to the "Circulation Day" site with at least one item that has been "out of circulation." In this way, the circle of giving and receiving is complete.

3. Habitat for Humanity is a wonderful non-profit organization that is providing housing for people around the world. Assisting this organization achieve its goals is a powerful way for a person to help others receive housing.

These three projects are indicative of the many possibilities that are before us if we are willing to look at needs as gifts. Helping people meet their tangible needs is important, but we must not stop with food, clothing, and shelter. This next step sows the seed for the end of poverty.

Going the Extra Mile

Many years ago I was lost in thought while mowing the grass. Something had happened that caused me to think about our system of welfare and public assistance. I wondered about the feelings of those who receive the assistance. Do they feel more or less when they are helped? What is the purpose of the welfare system? Obviously, it is a safety net in extreme cases, but what of the people who spend a lifetime on welfare? And what of the families who receive welfare payments or assistance for generations? Where is their opportunity to have their dreams realized? Where is their opportunity for education and meaningful employment and service?

As I pushed the lawnmower from one end of the yard to another, these kinds of thoughts pushed me to consider a balanced project not only for helping people to have food, shelter, and clothing, but for helping people discover the spiritual principles that can transform a life. I concluded that spiritual ideas and laws could be shared and people could experience them in a nonreligious way.

An idea came to mind that I have expressed in a limited way, but I believe it has possibilities. What if a "breakthrough class" was conducted with participants who were interviewed to determine their aptitude and willingness to break out of their limited situations? At every class, a specific amount of money would be given to help meet living expenses, and at the conclusion of the class a grant could be given that would help the person in the next stage of his or her life. The class would be an experience in which each person would become an explorer and researcher who puts to the test the prosperity principles and ideals. Interviewing and related job skills would also be taught as the students prepared themselves to enter the job market. Aptitude tests would be conducted in order to determine job training needs. After the class, the graduate would be assigned a "friend" who would serve as a support person during the time of transition from intellectually knowing the Truth to living the Truth.

Obviously, these are the thoughts of a man mowing the grass, but somewhere in the midst of them, there are seeds that could bear fruit. I have wondered about keeping track of the graduates as they began to apply the spiritual principles and skills they had learned. After five years, I wonder how many of them would be contributing members of society. What if we kept track of these people and then eventually told the story of their success to our government officials? When we go the extra mile with a project such as this, we must provide not only financial resources, but also human resources and caring, loving support. I believe this combination will make a difference.

In my dreams, I can see several hundred people standing in crowded congressional chambers to tell their stories. One would begin by saying that five years ago the group of unemployed individuals received tens of thousands of dollars of public assistance. Now they pay tens of thousands of dollars in taxes and, more important, are contributing members of society. They have broken through and are living not only the American dream, but lives of serenity and inner security.

Let us not war against poverty. Let us embrace it and enter a new era in which needs are seen as gifts and as an opportunity for the human family to discover the joy of giving and serving. Let us begin by helping people find food to eat, clothes to wear, and shelter from the cold—but we must not stop there. One more thing must be offered to them, and it is the discovery that God is their source and a consciousness that God is their supply.

SECTION
FOUR

A Forty-Day Guide to Prosperous Living

This section challenges you to put the principles of this book into practice in your daily life.

No prophet can tell us how long it will take to truly prosper. However, a spiritually rooted security and well-being are our destiny, so let the journey to no-needs begin. This section of the book will take a minimum of forty days to complete, but let us not be literal-minded. The number forty, whether it is forty days or forty years, symbolizes the time required to complete a task.

Our task is to open ourselves to Spirit and be willing to experience life

155

anew. A literal forty days may lie before us, but the greater journey is persistence leading to the discovery that
"the fields are already white for harvest."

DAY ONE

Today, I begin a partnership with God.

I cannot prosper alone. No one can. Without a relationship with God, there is no well-being and security. Hundreds of people may work with me, but unless I am in partnership with Spirit, true prosperity is just a dream.

Today I begin a partnership with God. Spirit is my full partner. An infinite wisdom is guiding me. All the resources necessary for success are available to me. I have no fear because God is my partner.

In the world, before someone becomes a partner, an offer of partnership is made. *In the space below, write an invitation to God to become your partner. Be sure to include what you are willing to give to the partnership.*

DAY TWO

Needs are not the issue.

Needs command my attention. They tell me how important they are and that they must be met. Sometimes they seem to be not only the issue, but the only issue. This is not true. However, when I consider times during which I felt great needs, I realize they were some of my most difficult periods of unrest and insecurity.

Consider a time in your life when you were consumed by what you did not have. It could have been a job, a lost love, or a feeling for which you longed. The possibilities are infinite. In the space below, indicate what you longed for and the emotions you experienced during this difficult time.

Let this remembrance remind you that needs are not the issue. Other things are at stake. As long as you focus upon the needs, you cannot prosper.

Day Three

God does not fulfill needs.

For thousands of years humankind has believed that God fulfills needs, and because of this belief, we have prayed and prayed. Sometimes it appears as though God has answered our prayers by giving us what we think we want. At other times it seems that God does not care about us, for our wishes are not granted. In fact, some people would strongly agree that God does not fulfill needs because their problems never go away even though they pray and pray and work and work.

Spiritual awareness reveals that God does not act through needs. Spirit's avenue of expression is an awareness of Itself. Joel Goldsmith said, "What God can do, God is doing." I love this statement, for it points to God's consistency and the remarkable way in which the universe is made.

What God can do, God is always doing. If God could fulfill even one need, all needs would be fulfilled. They would be taken care of, but we would be like spoiled children rather than spiritual beings awakened to our true nature.

Thank God, our wise Creator devised a universe

in which awareness of the Source is required rather than the emptiness of a need.

Today, rather than hold up your need to God, give God your attention and open yourself to a relationship with Spirit and the discovery that you are a spiritual being.

Day Four

God is the Source.

This is one of the foundation principles of this book—God is the Source. We say we believe it, but we wonder how people can starve to death if God is the Source. There is the implication that the Source should do something to meet the need.

Now I know this is not God's way, for what the Source can do, the Source is doing. It may seem as if God being the Source should be enough for me, but more is required of me—understanding and awareness.

In the same way that a recipe cannot feed me, so the Source does not give me nourishment. The recipe is not the cake; it is what makes the cake possible. It is the substance of the cake, for it stands under the finished form that is eaten. God, the Source, is that which stands under all form and makes possible the fulfillment of every need.

Today give thanks that God is the Source. Make no demands upon the Source; simply rejoice and give thanks.

DAY FIVE

A consciousness of God is supply.

This is the second foundation principle of this book. It is difficult for us to believe that something as unseen as a consciousness of God could be supply, but it is true. This is the great discovery that makes true prosperity possible. This understanding reveals our responsibility. Humankind would like to have God meet our needs, but even earthly parents try to teach their children responsibility, so that one day they will care for themselves.

Opening myself to a consciousness of Spirit is my responsibility. It is the first step not only to having my needs met, but also to discovering who I am. I can live on Earth in security, but the greater gift is an emerging relationship with God.

Today is another day of thanksgiving. Rejoice, for you now know one of the key elements of the universe and how the cosmos is devised. A consciousness of God is supply.

DAY SIX

Divine supply is available to me.

The earthly supply of money, credit, precious metals, and land is not available to everyone; however, all can prosper because everyone can awaken to an awareness of the Presence. This is the love of God in expression. It affirms that we are loved and cherished.

Even when I am in deep despair, bankrupt, or lost at sea with no visible means of support, I can become conscious of the Source. This awareness supplies my needs.

What is the first gift you receive when you become aware of God's presence?

What is the second gift?

The answer to each question can be found on the bottom of the next day's lesson.

DAY SEVEN

A consciousness of God is my daily bread. There is no need to hoard it.

It is fear that hoards and a consciousness of lack that believes supply must be stored for another day. In an earthly sense, it is acceptable to plan for retirement or to save money for a special use at a future time, but I refuse to believe I can store true supply for another day.

God must come to me fresh and new each day. Yesterday's manna cannot bring me security and supply my needs today. Yesterday's relationship with Spirit should be appreciated on the day it is given, but another day requires the unfoldment of a deeper, more loving relationship.

Give thanks that you must know your Source each day. This points you to a way of life of knowing God rather than having God fulfill your needs.

Are you willing to put aside yesterday's manna and experience a daily bread that is a deepened relationship with God?

The first gift is a sense of well-being and security.
The second gift is the meeting of our earthly needs.

DAY EIGHT

A consciousness of God cannot be limited.

Money cannot buy everything. If an automobile costs $20,000 and my credit will allow only the purchase of a $15,000 car, I cannot drive away with the more expensive vehicle. If I want to buy a $20 meal, but have only $5 in my pocket, I had better head for a fast-food restaurant. Money has its limitations, but a consciousness of God cannot be limited. It will take the shape necessary to meet the need.

World economic conditions impact the financial markets of many countries and influence interest rates that determine mortgage payments for a new home. A consciousness of God is untouched by economic conditions. This is why people prosper in the most adverse times. I am beginning to see the wisdom of God's plan and how a consciousness of the Source is better than money, credit, land, and precious metals.

Continue to work with this idea today by holding to this thought: *A consciousness of God is untouched by world economic conditions. When I am consciously one with God, I am untouched by the world.*

DAY NINE

A consciousness of God is available to everyone.

Earthly supply has its limitations. Some have it and some don't. Some people are born into immense wealth while others are born into deprivation. Some areas of the world have great natural resources while others seem devoid of valuable things, and yet the supply that prospers us in all ways is available to all.

Who cannot awaken to God's presence? This is the wonder of the divine plan. God is with me always, waiting for me to awaken. This realization takes away all of my excuses as to why I do not experience security and well-being.

In the space below, indicate some of your personal excuses for why you have not prospered. Are you willing to put them aside?

Day Ten

My supply is unaffected by earthly conditions.

My current supply is a consciousness of God, and it is unaffected by earthly conditions. It has not always been this way. In the past, my supply was more tangible.

List some examples of what you used to consider to be supply.

Now list some of the things that you used to believe affected your supply.

The fact is that earthly supply can be affected by many things. However, your supply is secure and untouched by such things. *How has this understanding changed your life?*

DAY ELEVEN

Awareness and acquisition are one.
Supply=Demand

One of the challenges of living a spiritual life is that the earthly life tugs at me so strongly. The world of appearances is always before me, and my five senses are constantly giving me information about a world I came to believe was real. This is one of the reasons why a life of prayer is so important. Prayer puts me in touch with another kingdom that the mystics say is real. In Truth, this kingdom is the foundation of all that appears.

This indwelling kingdom is more than thought, feeling, and image. It is the realm of Spirit, and it transcends these expressions of human faculties. It seems odd that simply becoming aware of this kingdom can change me and have such an impact on my earthly life, but this is the way the Creator devised the universe.

On Earth, there is a principle of supply and demand. As the demand for an item or resource increases, the supply must increase to meet it. Often the supply is controlled in a way that makes the price of the item or resource increase. People prosper financially through this process.

In the kingdom of God, it is different. Supply is always available, and nothing is withheld. Supply equals demand; awareness and acquisition are one. To become aware of something is to experience it. This principle can take many forms.

I remember a landscaped yard that Nancy and I admired as we took our walks around the neighborhood where we lived. We did none of the work of weeding and mowing, but we enjoyed the yard as much as the people who maintained it—maybe more! We did not pay the mortgage on the house, but it was ours, for it brought us joy and a great sense of beauty.

Is there something in your life that you do not literally own, but which is yours by awareness? If so, briefly describe it below.

Remember, awareness and acquisition are one, so give great attention to becoming more aware of God rather than trying to get what you think you want.

DAY TWELVE

Within me are barriers to a relationship with God.

It is clear. God is not withholding anything from me. Spirit is not withholding Itself from me. What I need is before me, but I see dimly. What I desire is within me, but I am not aware of it.

The Holy of Holies in the Temple of Israel was where God was supposed to dwell. There was a veil that hung from the ceiling before the Holy of Holies. A person could look into this part of the Temple, but could not see clearly. The veil represents a sense of separation between humanity and God. This was the veil that was torn when Jesus died on the cross. "Behold, the curtain of the temple was torn in two, from top to bottom" (Mt.27:51).

The veil or barrier can take many forms. For now, I do not concern myself with the exact nature of the veil that I have constructed between God and myself. It is only important to acknowledge that it is there.

Write a statement that acknowledges that there are barriers in you which stand between you and your ability to awaken to the Presence.

DAY THIRTEEN

Today I no longer judge by appearances.

Today's statement is an incredible one, but it is more a statement of the beginning of a journey than the end. I may strive to not judge by appearances today, but the day will come when appearances will rule my life again. When that time comes, this will be a good day to remember. Then I will be able to start again.

This is a day of sensitivity, a day to determine those things that cry out to be made powers in my life. If I do not turn within for guidance so I can judge rightly, these things will demand quick judgments and pretend that they are sources of wisdom.

During the course of this day, remain open and try to determine the things or circumstances that tend to cause you to judge by appearances. List them below and continue to be sensitive to them. In this way, you will be alert to times when a barrier to God might be erected.

DAY FOURTEEN

Today I stop thinking lack.

Today, like yesterday, is a day of sensitivity. It is wonderful when my mind is filled with abundance, faith, and security, but I learn more about my human nature when I become aware of the patterns of lack- and loss-thinking that are within me.

I will start this day by thinking positively, but I will not dismay if my thinking turns to what I do not have. I will learn from these thoughts.

The journey to positive, abundant thinking passes through a valley called thoughts of lack. If you pass through this valley today, determine the nature of these thoughts and their origin. *List them below and indicate what condition or situation in your life causes them to come to mind.*

DAY FIFTEEN

Today I am willing to forgive.

This is one of the most important tasks I can embark upon. Forgiveness of myself and others prepares me to experience the love God is. This experience prospers me in wonderful ways.

Notice that today it is not necessary to forgive, but only to be willing to forgive. Willingness is the beginning of transformation and a step I can take.

List below those individuals whom you are willing to forgive. Don't forget to include yourself if you must be forgiven. Instead of just listing the names of the people, write each name in the following statement: (Name of the person), I am willing to forgive you.

1.

2.

3.

4.

DAY SIXTEEN

A belief in possession is a block to prosperity.

The idea of possession seems so natural. It is part of the experience of most human beings. We possess many things. In fact, even children are said to have *their* toys. And those who have little or nothing often want to possess what others have.

However, possessions bind me to the Earth. It is the human being that possesses many things. As a spiritual being, I possess nothing. I have all I need as a part of my spiritual nature. The things of the world are a burden. In my heart, I know this is true, but there also must be balance.

Society's economic system is partially based upon the idea of possession. There are bills of sale and deeds. Religious orders "protect" their monks from such encumbrances, but the order owns land, buildings, and other things necessary to carry on the work.

Balance lies not in giving away all that I have, but in remembering that, as a citizen of the world, I am a spiritual being whose identity is in God rather than in something I can call my own. I can still own my home yet not be possessed by it. The key is knowing who I am.

In the space below, formulate your own statement that expresses your willingness to be free of possession.

Day Seventeen

Poverty is believing earthly things make me rich and secure.

The human viewpoint is that I am poor when I have little money and few earthly possessions. The mystical viewpoint is that I am poor when I am without a consciousness of God, and that my poverty worsens when I believe earthly things make me rich.

Those who experience the closer walk with God yearn for that which endures and cannot be taken away by thieves or by death. For too long, I have been poor—not because I had little, but because I did not want what makes me rich, a relationship with Spirit.

Now I am prepared for the richness of the Presence. *Carry this statement throughout this day: Dear God, my Friend, without You I am poor, no matter how much I have. With You, I am rich, no matter how little I have.*

DAY EIGHTEEN

I deserve the kingdom of heaven.

Reading or speaking this affirmation should bring us a sense of humility and a certain degree of healthy disbelief. Let us not make the mistake of thinking that we deserve to experience the Presence because of what we have done. We deserve a relationship with Spirit not because of what we have done, but because of what God is doing.

It is arrogance that causes us to claim the kingdom as if we would go to court to get what is ours if it was not given. Remember, the kingdom is an awareness of God, a growing, conscious relationship with Spirit. Let us not claim it; let us give ourselves to it.

You deserve the kingdom because God created a universe in which you are an integral part. You are an avenue through which Spirit expresses Itself. Do not lift yourself high because God has made you in this way. Make yourself low, and Spirit will show you your perfect place.

Even if these ideas are foreign to your way of thinking, spend this day without contention with them, and ponder these questions during the day: *Where was I, what was I doing when God offered me the kingdom? Is it true that only the humble deserve the kingdom?*

Day Nineteen

I receive according to my capacity to receive.

There is much that I deserve and much that is being offered to me, but when my arms are full of things, I have little capacity to receive. Today pretend that you have been asked by a prophet to go and gather many containers from your neighbors. Soon the prophet will begin to fill the containers with wondrous treasures.

In the story of Elisha, the widow, and the oil (2 Kings 4:1–7), when there were no more containers to fill, the oil stopped flowing. The widow reached her capacity to receive. Through the eighteen days that you have been working with this section of the book, you are aware that it is not oil or earthly things which are important. You are opening yourself to a closer walk with God.

List the containers that you will bring to the prophet, not to be filled with oil but as a symbol of your willingness to experience the Presence. For instance, one of the containers might be humility, another prayer. List at least "twelve containers" that you will bring to the prophet.

1.

2.

3.

4.

5.

6.

7.

8.

9.

10.

11.

12.

DAY TWENTY

When I am aware of God, asking ceases.

The Bible says again and again that I must ask. I thought I was being told to ask for earthly things I needed. Now I know I was being told to ask for God.

Children know the power of asking, for when they have received what they want, the asking ceases. A cookie is desired, and while it is being eaten, there is no asking.

The human compulsion to ask or even to plead is strong. We seem to know the principle, "Ask, and it will be given you" (Mt. 7:7). Let us also know that when the gift is received, asking is no more.

Look for this sign in your life. When you are consciously one with God, you will not ask for anything. How could you? You have your heart's desire. Whenever there is the need to ask, you are not yet consciously one with God.

DAY TWENTY-ONE

A rich one has no needs.

I have desired riches. Oh, to be rich . . . what a gift it would be! It is true. To be rich is a great gift, but it does not mean having vast sums of money; it means being totally free from the world.

The rich person does not necessarily have many things; he or she has one thing—an awareness of God. This is all that is needed. Asking has ceased. Total fulfillment sweeps over the soul.

Reread the above two paragraphs twice in the morning, twice in the afternoon, and twice in the evening. Whenever you have your daily prayer time, ponder the inner meaning of these words and let total fulfillment sweep over your soul.

DAY TWENTY-TWO

The no-need state is my natural state.

For most of us for many years to come, our lives will swing between periods of asking and periods of fulfillment. This is natural and a part of the spiritual journey, but let it be known that the no-need state is my most natural state. Most likely I am far from my destiny, but one day I will live in a perpetual state of no-needs. If I am still on the Earth, all of my earthly needs will be met without having to make their fulfillment the object of my existence.

This is the challenge of the spiritual life. There is a way of living, a way of being, in which earthly experience flows from my spiritual life. I do not need to give earthly matters great attention because they are added things. I will be able to fully dedicate myself to the spiritual life, and all will be well.

There are many signs of the coming of this kingdom and way of life, and one of them is the no-need state. Contentment and fulfillment herald this way of life. I look for them, not in the world, but in my relationship with God.

Day Twenty-Three

Only the rich enter the kingdom of heaven.

I have thought that only the poor could enter the kingdom, or at least I *questioned* the possibility of the rich knowing the kingdom of God. Their focus is usually so earthly. Now I have a new definition of what it is to be rich. It is to have God—it is to experience the Presence. When I am rich in this way, I am in the kingdom of heaven.

Determine today that you will be rich. Please understand that you cannot make this happen, but you can open yourself to the experience. Day by day, you can give yourself to true riches—the experience of the Presence.

Make a covenant that you will pray each day for the next forty days. Let your prayers be primarily silence and waiting. Let the words you speak or the thoughts that move through your mind be a yearning for conscious oneness with God.

These prayers are always answered.

DAY TWENTY-FOUR

Richness is determined by what I do with what I have.

Is someone rich who has vast sums of money but keeps it locked away in a vault? Is this person rich even though he or she does nothing with this immense wealth? Perhaps the individual lives in poverty instead of in opulence.

Money is inert; it is nothing without us. It has little meaning unless I use it in constructive ways. The simple Truth is that richness is determined by what I do with what I have. It does not matter how much money I have or what my talents may be. *Use* determines whether I am a rich and purposeful person.

If I use the money and the talents I have only for my benefit, I am not rich. The truly rich reach out to the world. They make it a better place by what they do and who they are.

Look at what you have—your financial resources, your time, and your talents. How much of each is used on yourself and how much of your time, talents, and resources is used for the common good? On the following lines, write the percentage of your time, talents, and resources that is used for God's glory.

_____ % time   _____% talents

_____ % resources

What does this tell you about how rich you are?

DAY TWENTY-FIVE

Manifestation is none of my business.

When I am of the Earth, manifestation is my primary business. I am concerned with what is happening in my life. I take thought about what I shall eat and drink and wear.

As my spiritual life is born and begins to grow, eventually, manifestation is no longer my business. I refuse to bring spiritual principles to bear upon my earthly experience. I willingly put to the test the ideal that Jesus taught. If I will seek first the kingdom, then manifestation in its many forms will be added to me without making it my primary business.

God is my primary business. Giving myself to God is my work. It seems natural that if I do this, my earthly needs will be met. This is a basic principle I must put to the test.

I am immensely interested in your experience as you adopt this way of life. Write to me, and tell me about how your life changes because you seek the kingdom and take no thought for your life.

Please turn down the corner of this page as a reminder if you would like to write me about the results of your "experiment" with this mystical ideal. Please write to Jim Rosemergy, P.O. Box 2113, Lee's Summit, MO 64063.

Day Twenty-Six

I cannot serve God and mammon.

Here is the challenge. I am a spiritual being living in a manifest world that commands my attention. Constantly my five senses send me information about the world. Often because of this deluge of input, I come to believe that the outer world is what is most important. I want the world to conform to my desires, but usually I conform to it.

One thing is sure—I cannot serve God and the world at the same time. There are not two options. I am not aware of a principle that states I will deepen my relationship with God if I seek the "good life." I have never heard it said that if I seek the added things I will also have God.

In Truth, if I seek God I will have it all. This does not mean that God is to be the avenue through which I acquire earthly riches. When I have God, I will not give undue attention to my world. God will be first, the world will be in its place, and there will be joy.

Choose this day whom you will serve, God or mammon. Write a statement that indicates which you have chosen to serve.

DAY TWENTY-SEVEN

Manifestation begins in Silence.

It is good to live a spiritual life, but I am also living in the world. Even mystics have bills to pay. Yes, they do, but they also realize that manifestation begins in Silence. Silence, an experience of the Presence, is without thought, feeling, or imagination. It usually lasts for only a moment, but like any state of consciousness, it will manifest itself as my experience.

The first manifestation of the Silence is usually a thought, feeling, or image. Next, the physical body may be healed or restored in some way. Ideas may come. Some course of action may be revealed. I become more sensitive to my outer world and no longer miss opportunities for growth because I have not recognized them.

Imagine only a moment in the Silence; only a brief encounter with Spirit in a state of pure silence and my life is changed forever. Human relationships are healed. New ideas rise from within me. Latent talents are revealed. Peace passing understanding floods my soul. Joy without cause is mine. The strength to go on in difficult times is available to me.

Ponder these things in your heart, for this is God's way. First, there is oneness in Spirit, and then your world is filled not only with opportunity and added things, it is filled with God.

DAY TWENTY-EIGHT

Thanksgiving prepares me for the kingdom of heaven.

On a previous day I prepared for the kingdom by giving what I have been given: time, talents, and financial resources. Today I prepare for the kingdom by giving thanks.

Thanksgiving fills my soul with an awareness of what *is* rather than a longing for what has not yet come. It reminds me that there is no lack in the kingdom and in my life, so I look at my world with a fresh vision.

Today make a list of your blessings and put them in three groupings: people, physical things, and spiritual things.

List four people for whom you are thankful.

1.

2.

3.

4.

List seven physical things for which you are thankful.

1.

2.

3.

4.

5.

6.

7.

List twelve spiritual "things" for which you are thankful.

1.

2.

3.

4.

5.

6.

7.

8.

9.

10.

11.

12.

DAY TWENTY-NINE

Today I bless my bills and their payment.

Today is a simple day of action. Hopefully, the practice of blessing your bills and your payment will not be just for today but for as long as it takes for you to adopt a thankful attitude when handling money. The days of bemoaning the payment of bills are gone. Money is an earthly symbol of the supply, which is an awareness of the Presence.

Place your bills before you along with your payment. In the space below, write a simple blessing that expresses an attitude of thankfulness. Hold each bill or invoice and payment between your hands. Hold your hands prayerfully and speak aloud the blessing you have written. Do this whenever you pay a bill until thankfulness is a natural part of your way of being.

DAY THIRTY

Today I am aware of my blessings.

Today is another simple day of action. Thanksgiving is one of the doorways to a consciousness of God. In Truth, when I am aware of Spirit, I am thankful. How could there not be thankfulness when I am one with the One?

There are many forms of thankfulness and many paths that lead me to this wonderful way of life. Today I am going to journey upon one of the paths. I am going to give thanks for my blessings. Essentially, this practice is a repeat of Day Twenty-Eight. This important pathway to God is stressed again in order to bring a sense of thankfulness to mind daily.

Today I am giving thanks for my blessings, but the day will come when thankfulness will rise up within me whether or not there is something to be thankful for in my outer world. Eventually, I will always walk a path of thankfulness with God.

This evening before you go to sleep, write what has blessed you the most today.

Day Thirty-One

Prosperity's demonstration is giving.

Most people believe they demonstrate prosperity when they receive. This is not true; it has never been true. Prosperity's demonstration is giving.

There is joy when I receive a gift, but the greater joy is giving a gift. Today I lay plans to put this statement to the test. Either it will prove true or it will not.

Plan to make a prosperity demonstration by giving an anonymous gift to someone. Determine who will receive the gift and write his or her name in the space provided.

Determine what the gift will be and indicate what it is.

Then give the gift anonymously and determine for yourself if prosperity's demonstration is giving. Write your conclusion below.

DAY THIRTY-TWO

Giving is not loss.

It seems so obvious. When I give something away, I no longer have it. This is true. However, there is no loss. A seed has been planted.

God has devised the universe in a way in which giving is not loss, but an invitation to Spirit to bless me with a greater awareness of Itself. When I give, the greatest blessing I can receive is an expanded awareness of Spirit. Every genuine act of giving receives this gift.

Give, and watch for your expanded awareness of God. This consciousness is your supply and will bless you and the world. Mark this page and return to it when you sense an expanded awareness has come upon you. Was it a feeling of well-being or security? Did an idea come to you? Did fear of the future dissipate? The possibilities are many, for a consciousness of God is made known in varied ways.

DAY THIRTY-THREE

Giving is a matter of spiritual understanding and values.

Prosperity's demonstration comes easily to those who know their source. Spiritual understanding demands certain actions, for when I am spiritually aware I have no fear. There is no concern for to-morrow. I know the law of giving and receiving and that giving is not loss, nor is it gain. Giving is life in expression in the same way that our breath's exhalation and a flower's releasing its fragrance to the air are life in expression. Giving is something I must do. It does not depend upon what I have, but whether I have spiritual understanding and value it.

Giving to God's work is a priority for people who understand the transformative power of knowing God. I do not place myself and my needs above the need for spiritual awakening. However, most people have had a time in their lives when they did not give because their values were askew. They said they could not give, but they used their money for frivolous evenings of entertainment. Please realize there is nothing wrong with a frivolous evening on the town unless it causes us to be unable to contribute to the unfoldment of God's work.

There is nothing to do today specifically, but it is important to reexamine your values, for giving is a matter of spiritual understanding and values.

DAY THIRTY-FOUR

Giving allows me to become aware of the Presence.

Giving is one of the great paradoxes because it appears to yield nothing. In fact, when I judge by appearances, I have less than what I had before. How wonderful it is that our Creator has designed a universe in which giving is a blessing.

There are many potential blessings that can come into my life because I am a cheerful giver, but I must not always focus on what is made manifest in my life. The Truth is that manifestation has its origin in me. When I give, I open myself not so much to manifestation as to an awareness of the Presence. This is the first gift of giving. This God-consciousness then is made manifest in ways that I cannot predict, but in ways which are blessings not only to me but to others.

Has there been a time in your life when some wonderful form of manifestation took you totally by surprise? Consider an instance when you were not only blessed, but others were as well. This is a sign that you have received the true gift of your giving, for you have awakened to the Presence.

DAY THIRTY-FIVE

I give because it is my nature.

There is a rite of passage of giving. At first, I do not give. Next, I give out of a sense of guilt and then out of duty. Eventually, I give in order to receive, and finally, I give because it is my nature. Today I do not condemn myself because of my reason for giving, but I am willing to progress until I give because it is my nature.

Has there ever been a time in your life when you wanted to give but did not? You felt the desire to give but for logical reasons you did not. It may have been that the desire you felt was a movement of Spirit. Bringing it to mind sensitizes you to the feeling. If it is God calling you to express your divine nature, you will be able to respond differently than you have in the past.

Read this day's thoughts three times today: in the morning, at lunch time, and before you go to bed. By giving attention to this idea, you invite into your experience an opportunity for you to give because it is your nature. When that time comes, return to this page and describe what happened.

DAY THIRTY-SIX

Today I look for opportunities to give.

While I am waiting to feel the inner movement of Spirit calling me to give because it is my nature, I will look for opportunities to give that come to me every day. I will not think solely of opportunities to give money. There will be times when I can share encouragement, ideas, an experience, or even vegetables from my garden.

Record the various categories of giving that come to you between now and the 40th day of this prospering process into which you have entered.

DAY THIRTY-SEVEN

Ideas are a bridge between the kingdom of heaven and my daily life.

Sometimes the kingdom of heaven, a consciousness of God, seems far away. How can something so abstract and absolute have an impact on my life? Through the years, I have heard many people say that they thought prayer was impractical. Action, not stillness, is required for daily living, they said.

The Truth *is* nothing is more practical than prayer because it ultimately leads to an awareness of Spirit. This consciousness then manifests itself in ways that directly impact daily life. For instance, ideas begin to rise out of the kingdom.

Ideas are a bridge between the kingdom of God and my daily life. Ideas are like the air I breathe because they cannot be held in my hands. They, like the kingdom, seem to have no substance to them, but they are the foundation of all that appears.

Today there is no need to look for ideas. It is enough that I accept the concept that ideas are a bridge between the kingdom of heaven and the world. When an idea comes upon me, it is evidence that I have contact with Spirit, and spiritual consciousness is beginning to be made manifest in and as my life.

Day Thirty-Eight

Today I am open to prospering ideas.

Today, pray and then watch for ideas that emerge from within. Sometimes you will receive an idea in prayer and meditation. At other times, it will come when you least expect it. The key is recognizing the idea when it comes. Usually, it will require action, and the path to its fulfillment in the world will not be evident at first, but with persistence and the willingness to act boldly, the manifestation will come.

Let today's thought be the initial focus of your prayer and meditation. Record any ideas that come to you.

DAY THIRTY-NINE

I put God first.

If I want to prosper, if I want to be fully alive, I must put God first. Earlier in the book, this practice was described as tithing, but it is much more than giving money to a channel of one's spiritual good. Tithing is a consciousness of putting God first, which eventually becomes the center of my life. It is expressed as I give money, but also when I give the gifts of my time and talents.

It is crucial that I put God first in my life. Perhaps a good place to begin is to become aware of those areas of my life where God is not first.

The following questions will help you determine if you are or are not putting God first.

Do you tithe your income?

How much of your time is dedicated to prayer and meditation, reading and study of spiritual subjects, and service to others? (Please realize that your service to others may not be a part of your job but is expressed as your willingness to spontaneously help or support others in times of need.)

Have you discovered your talent? If you have not, it is time to call it forth by expressing your willingness to use it in service to God. If you know what your talent is, are you using it for God's glory?

Based on the insights you received by answering the questions, write in the space below your next steps in adopting a way of life that puts God first.

DAY FORTY

Today I begin my debt-free life.

Today is a glorious day, for it is not just the end of a forty-day period of study and reflection, it is the beginning of a debt-free life.

This does not mean I will never owe money to an individual or institution again. Instead, it expresses my willingness to live life free from thoughts of lack and deprivation. More important, it is my commitment to experience the Presence as my source and supply.

Give thanks and rejoice in your persistence to give yourself to this forty-day process. However, do not think that it is complete. The ideas and practices you have experienced are not to be put behind you but incorporated into your life. This is the next question you must answer: How will your life be different because of the commitment you have made to the mystical life? As you answer this question in the days to come, live the life that is revealed to you.

CONCLUSION

Mystics have bills to pay, but so do we. The bills are not the real issue. Life's quest is more than making ends meet: it is living within the divine circle that is oneness with God. When we know this, we are *in* the world, but not of it.

I hope that you have caught a glimpse of this world and know that a place has been prepared for you within it. The time to experience this life of oneness with God is now. The signs that you are assuming your rightful place are few.

There will be a simplicity to your life. The need for more and more things will wane. Your most basic need is an awareness of God. Much of what you have will support this yearning of your soul.

You will live in thankfulness, not just for what you have, but because thankfulness is your way of life. You give thanks for the life that has been revealed to you.

You will be free of the burden of possession. This does not mean that you will have nothing because you have given it away. It means that what you have will be yours to use while you are here. You will "own" nothing in a cosmic sense, for what does a spiritual being need? If you have anything, it will be an appreciation of the wonder, mystery, and beauty of the world.

You will be a servant of the many. Although there will be joy in your soul, there will also be sorrow until all people live life in this way.

Teacher's Guide

If you are planning to teach or study *Even Mystics Have Bills to Pay* with a group, a Teacher's Guide is available for your use. For information about the guide, write to Jim and Nancy Rosemergy at P.O. Box 2113, Lee's Summit, MO 64063.

My hope is that as many people as possible will have the opportunity to learn about the mystical approach to prosperity, security, and well-being. It is my joy to provide supportive materials to help fellow seekers live a life of oneness with God. Not only am I committed to assisting those who want to learn about this special way of life, I am also dedicated to helping those who would help others find their true Source.

ABOUT THE AUTHOR

Jim Rosemergy serves as executive vice president of Unity School of Christianity at its world headquarters in Unity Village, Missouri. Jim also serves on the Unity Movement Advisory Council, a joint committee of the Association of Unity Churches and Unity School of Christianity.

Jim was born on July 13, 1947, in Elizabeth City, North Carolina. Because his father was in the military, he moved frequently, going to twelve different schools in twelve years. He lived in numerous places along the Gulf and East coasts, from Mobile, Alabama, to Cape Cod, Massachusetts. An athletic boy and natural leader, he found himself excelling at tennis, captaining his tennis team at Old Dominion College (now Old Dominion University), where he also earned a B.S. in chemistry. Jim saw combat in North Vietnam as a naval aviator and flew more than one hundred missions.

Reverend Rosemergy was ordained a Unity minister in 1976. He pioneered a ministry in Raleigh, North Carolina, that grew from eighteen people to over three hundred in seven years, with an emphasis on prayer (an activity which continues to be at the heart of his ministry). Next, Jim served Unity Church of Truth in Spokane, Washington, where his emphasis was on spiritual awakening and assisting people in their quests for purpose and meaning in life.

Prior to returning to Unity Village, Jim served as senior minister at the cofounders' church, Unity Temple on the Plaza, in Kansas City, Missouri. In 1987–88, he was elected president of the Association of Unity Churches.

Jim is also a writer of numerous articles and poems, as well as nine books. His column "The Spiritual Journey" appears monthly in *Unity Magazine*. His books include *The Sacred Human, A Closer Walk With God,* and *The Quest for Meaning*.

Jim and Nancy, his wife of over twenty-nine years, have two grown sons, Jamie and Ben.

Printed in the U.S.A.   0182-0815-75C-6-00